About Island Press

Since 1984, the nonprofit organization Island Press has been stimulating, shaping, and communicating ideas that are essential for solving environmental problems worldwide. With more than 1,000 titles in print and some 30 new releases each year, we are the nation's leading publisher on environmental issues. We identify innovative thinkers and emerging trends in the environmental field. We work with world-renowned experts and authors to develop cross-disciplinary solutions to environmental challenges.

Island Press designs and executes educational campaigns, in conjunction with our authors, to communicate their critical messages in print, in person, and online using the latest technologies, innovative programs, and the media. Our goal is to reach targeted audiences—scientists, policy makers, environmental advocates, urban planners, the media, and concerned citizens—with information that can be used to create the framework for long-term ecological health and human well-being.

Island Press gratefully acknowledges major support from The Bobolink Foundation, Caldera Foundation, The Curtis and Edith Munson Foundation, The Forrest C. and Frances H. Lattner Foundation, The JPB Foundation, The Kresge Foundation, The Summit Charitable Foundation, Inc., and many other generous organizations and individuals.

The opinions expressed in this book are those of the author(s) and do not necessarily reflect the views of our supporters.

Praise for *A Year of Compassion*

"This book had me from page one, from the concept that our goal is a life of compassion—imperfect, of course, but brilliant and beautiful and necessary all the same. And these weekly focus points are agreeably accessible. They make sense in real life, as they help us create a kinder world."

—Victoria Moran, author of *Main Street Vegan* and *Age Like a Yogi*

"A masterclass in living intentionally. Colleen Patrick-Goudreau offers practical, actionable advice that empowers each of us to make small changes with profound impacts—for animals, the planet, and ourselves. This book is a gift to anyone striving for a kinder, more sustainable world."

—Kathy Freston, author of *Quantum Wellness*, *Veganist*, and *The Lean*

"*A Year of Compassion* is a roadmap for anyone who dreams of making a meaningful impact. Colleen Patrick-Goudreau shows that small, mindful choices can lead to profound change—for ourselves, the animals, and the planet."

—Paul Shapiro, CEO of The Better Meat Co. and author of *Clean Meat*

"If you want to make a difference while living a healthier, more meaningful life, read this book. Colleen Patrick-Goudreau offers friendly, inviting, and deeply impactful ideas to forge a truly compassionate life."

—Zoe Weil, President of the Institute for Humane Education and author of *The Solutionary Way*

A YEAR OF COMPASSION

52 Weeks of Living Zero-Waste, Plant-Based, and Cruelty-Free

Colleen Patrick-Goudreau

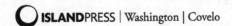

ISLANDPRESS | Washington | Covelo

All rights reserved under International and Pan-American Copyright Conventions. No part of this book may be reproduced in any form or by any means without permission in writing from the publisher: Island Press, 2000 M Street, NW, Suite 480-B, Washington, DC 20036-3319.

Note: This book is written for informational purposes only and is not intended to diagnose, treat, cure, or prevent any condition or disease. Please consult with your physician or healthcare specialist regarding how the recommendations made in this book may fit with your individual needs.

Library of Congress Control Number: 2024945783

All Island Press books are printed on environmentally responsible materials.

Manufactured in the United States of America
10 9 8 7 6 5 4 3 2 1

Keywords: animal rescue, animal rights, animal welfare, carbon-neutral, conservation, green living, healthy eating, low-carbon, meatless, nutrition, reuse and reduce, sustainability, veganism, waste-free, well-being

To Mom.
You started it.

CONTENTS

When I became vegan in 1999, my goal was not to be vegan. My goal was to be compassionate.

I wasn't looking to join a club, adopt a label, or signal a virtue. I was just trying to not hurt animals.

I had set out on this journey several years before having read John Robbins's book *Diet for a New America*, confronting for the first time the animal cruelty in the meat industry. And so, when I was twenty years old, I stopped eating land animals and eventually aquatic animals.

I became vegetarian.

All of this, however, was really just a natural progression of a journey that had begun when I was a child—a child who loved animals.

I have always had a deep empathy for animals and loved being around them, but I don't think I was so different from other children. Most are taught by adults to be kind to animals, to read their reactions, and to respect their space. Praised and rewarded when we're gentle, scolded and corrected when we're not, we learn early on that animals feel the same pain, fear, loneliness, sadness, happiness, excitement, and affection as we do. But more than that, both subtly and overtly we're taught that animals are an integral, instrumental, and indispensable part of who we are and who we are becoming.

When we are children, most of the clothing we're dressed in and the rooms we sleep in are decorated with depictions of animals—kittens, puppies, ducks, bunnies. Our childhood blankets, pillowcases, wallpaper, cribs, beds, backpacks, lunch boxes, plates, bowls, and cups—most are embellished with images and illustrations of baby lambs, baby pigs, baby elephants, baby birds. Plush toys and stuffed animals adorn our beds and become our comfort and constant companions.

Most of the games we play and the toys we cherish feature animal characters or animal themes. Books, films, television shows, and educational tools not only use animals to teach us about animals, but also use animals to teach us our most fundamental skills: how to count, how to read, how to spell, and how to talk.

Through fables and folklore, songs and parables, animals teach us how to interact with others, how to express emotions, and how to be kind. We're brought to the zoo to admire animals, we're dressed up as animals at Halloween, and many of us live with companion animals, whether they be dogs, cats, rabbits, gerbils, or goldfish. In every aspect of our lives, animals are intimately and inextricably part of our identity and development.

And while not every child necessarily has the desire to be in the company of animals as I did, most children are deeply distressed when they see an animal suffering or scared, even if it's a fictional, animated cartoon character. What child doesn't cry when Bambi loses his mother, when Wilbur grieves for Charlotte, when Simba finds the lifeless body of his father? I certainly did. I was also the child who intervened when actual animals were injured or stray, and I wept uncontrollably if I saw any animal neglected, abused, or abandoned.

What I didn't quite realize was that, at the same time, I was being fed the meat, milk, and eggs of animals—animals no different from the ones I was moved to help or was brought to the zoo to pet or whose likenesses ornamented my dresses and toys. Already deeply entrenched in social norms and cultural traditions, I was eating everything that walked or swam or flew, and I mitigated my guilt with justifications, especially as I got older.

Over time, the compassion that had been so instinctual in me as a child had become tempered in me as an adult—not in a way that made me hurt anyone directly but in ways that made me willfully blind toward my consumption of animals and the suffering I caused them as a result. I consciously shielded myself from what I knew I couldn't bear, and I unconsciously built a neat little wall to fortify my heart.

But even walls have fissures, and it's only a matter of time before they break down. I read one book, then another, and before I knew it, I was inspired to stop eating anything that came out of or off of an animal.

I became vegan.

I'm struck by how funny that phrase can sound—"to become vegan." We say an acorn becomes an oak tree, or a seed becomes a flower, or a caterpillar becomes a butterfly, and we can easily imagine how different they look before and after their transformation, but what does it mean to become vegan? What did I become when I became vegan? Something new? Something altered? Something else? How so? Prior to becoming vegan, I was already a compassionate person living a compassionate life. In my interactions with people and animals, I tried to be kind, caring, and good.

But, in reality, as evidenced by the cognitive dissonance I felt, those values weren't being fully reflected in my behavior. I would never have intentionally hurt another living being, but I was paying others to do it for me, behind closed doors where I didn't have to see.

So for me, when I became vegan, I didn't become something different as much as I became something more authentic, where my values of compassion and kindness were made manifest. Where my ethics aligned with my behavior. Where my daily choices became a reflection of my deepest values. The compassion that compelled me to save an injured bluebird when I was eight or take in a stray dog when I was twelve was the same compassion that compelled me to spare the animals designated as "food" when I was twenty. The recipients were different, but the compassion was just the same.

And so, I prefer to say that I didn't become vegan as much as I removed the blocks to the compassion that had always been inside of me, the compassion I believe is in all of us, the compassion we sacrifice in favor of conformity, convenience, and culture.

Of course, it's a lot more succinct to say, "I became vegan," but I make this distinction, because too often veganism is characterized as a goal to attain, a badge to wear, a destination to reach—when that's not the point at all.

Becoming vegan is not the *end*. It's the *means* to an end. And that end, that goal, is compassion: to live in such a way that doesn't intentionally cause harm—to ourselves or anyone else. So far, I've only been talking about veganism as a means of reflecting compassion for animals, but of course abstaining from meat, dairy, and eggs is also a means of reflecting compassion for ourselves and our loved ones. Whole books and countless peer-reviewed studies have made the case that eating a plant-based diet is the most beneficial thing we can do for our health.

The point is that if we see veganism—or plant-based eating—as the goal rather than as the means to attaining our goals (of compassion or wellness), we get hung up on ideology and rules, doctrines and dogma, perfection and purity. In other words, I don't aspire to be as vegan as I can be. Rather, I aspire to be as compassionate as I can be. Compassion is my goal. Wellness is my goal. Being vegan—eating plants and not animals—is just the most effective and effortless way I have found to achieve those goals.

But living compassionately isn't just about abstaining from meat, dairy, and eggs. My desire to avoid causing harm to animals extends to all animals—to those languishing in laboratories, circuses, cages, and fur farms; to those who are trapped, poisoned, shot, or abused; to those who are endangered, threatened, or exploited; to those whose habitats are dwindling, polluted, or dangerous. And so, just as quickly as I stopped eating animal products, I naturally and effortlessly found myself uncomfortable with wearing, using, or exploiting animals in any way. I naturally and effortlessly found myself wanting to live as lightly on this earth as possible—not seeking perfection or purity but progress and purpose. Being an ambassador of compassion meant being a steward of the Earth.

And so, soon after we became vegan, my husband and I began composting our food and yard scraps, relying both on our home composters as well as our city services. Eventually, we rerouted our plumbing and bought three 300-gallon rain tanks, enabling us to irrigate all of our gardens with gray water and rain-water. (We live in a drought-prone state, after all.) We purposefully live where we can walk everywhere, and when we do drive, we have just one car—a 100 percent electric vehicle. We installed solar panels on our roof to harness renew-able energy, and in an effort to reduce excess packaging, we buy most of our dry goods from a local bulk store, avoiding unnecessary packaging when possible. We use canvas bags for our groceries and wash and reuse any plastic bags that come into our home.

Not perfect, but not bad.

And yet, despite these efforts, a few years ago, I decided I wanted to do more, which led me to make additional changes in our lifestyle—both for myself and my husband—deepening our commitment to sustainability at home and in our daily lives.

I became "zero waste."

The first time I heard the term "zero waste" was in 2006, when my city of Oakland adopted its zero-waste policy in relation to its waste management. In fact, the term "zero waste" has its roots in Oakland as well; it originated in the 1970s when chemist Paul Palmer founded a company aimed at repurposing surplus chemicals from the electronics industry. Palmer defined *zero waste* as the systematic approach to resource management that seeks to prevent waste from being created in the first place. This involves designing systems and processes that maximize the reuse, recycling, and recovery of materials to minimize or eliminate waste. The goal is to create a closed-loop system where all resources are utilized effectively, and nothing is wasted.

Inspiring to be sure, but when I dug deeper, it became clear that zero waste is not just about what manufacturers, governments, and individuals do; it's about how we *think*. Zero waste is a philosophy, a perspective, an orientation that shapes the way we see the world, our place in it, and our relationship to it. Zero waste is, indeed, about taking such actions as recycling, restoring, repairing, repurposing, and reusing, but it's the zero-waste *mindset* that frames, shapes, and inspires these behaviors, making them feel achievable, satisfying, and effortless.

Just as being vegan was not about signaling my virtue or attaining perfection, neither is being zero waste. Just as the *goal* isn't to be vegan (the *goal* is to be compassionate; the *goal* is to be healthy), the *goal* here isn't to be zero waste. The goal is to minimize harmful environmental impacts of human activities, conserve natural resources, preserve biodiversity, and protect ecosystems for current and future generations. Adopting sustainable, "zero-waste" practices is the way to achieve that goal.

My journey of compassion thus far has been enlightening, empowering, overwhelming, exhilarating, and affirming. When I began living according to compassion, i.e., reflecting my deepest values in my daily behavior, the dissonance and discord I once felt simply fell away and was replaced by a deep sense of peace. I'm tempted to say that in doing so I returned to the innocent compassion of my childhood, but that's not the whole truth of it. When I became willing to look at how I was contributing to violence against animals I found a deeper place, a place of conscious compassion, where my eyes and heart are open not because of what I *don't* know, but because of what I *do* know. Choosing intentional awareness over willful blindness has deepened and amplified my commitment to living compassionately, the guiding principle of my life and this book.

When I first became aware of the atrocities committed against animals, I immersed myself in every book, every article, every bit of content offering solutions and ways to make a difference. I voraciously devoured books with such titles as *101 Ways to Save Animals* and *500 Ways to Help the Planet*. In my eagerness to alleviate suffering, I dove in and immediately started making changes in the foods I ate, the products I bought, the companies I supported (or boycotted), and the organizations I donated to. While I couldn't possibly implement every one of the hundreds of suggestions, many of these behaviors stuck and became habits.

The good news is that there are indeed millions of things we can do to manifest our values of compassion and wellness; the bad news is that they're not all equally effective. Quantity doesn't necessarily mean quality.

A Year of Compassion isn't about doing *more*. It's about doing *better*. It's not about acting *harder*. It's about acting *smarter*.

The earliest draft of this book imagined it filled with *daily* directives rather than *weekly*, but upon reflection (and direction from my very skilled and experienced editor), we landed on 52 weeks of actions rather than 365 days. We humans tend to do *nothing* when we think we have to do *everything*, so I've prioritized the most impactful, measurable, and effective actions we can take.

But living compassionately is not only about *doing*. How we spend our time and money is also contingent on how we *think* and what we *believe*, so some of what you'll read in the following chapters also has to do with shifting our perspective, changing our perceptions, orienting our mindset, and sharpening the lens through which we see the world. This will not only make behavioral changes more enjoyable and sustainable, it will also make them feel less arduous and more effortless. Mahatma Gandhi said it best: "Your beliefs become your thoughts, your thoughts become your words, your words become your actions, your actions become your habits, your habits become your values, your values become your destiny."

Finally, aspiring to live compassionately and healthfully is about *progress*, not perfection. Being imperfect people in an imperfect world, we are bound to make mistakes, struggle, and even fail in some aspects of this adventure, but to do nothing at all because we can't do everything is nonsensical and self-defeating. Creating attainable goals and adopting a mindset of intention rather than perfection will make the journey exciting rather than daunting. The main thing is to start where you are and get support along the way. That's what I'm here for.

Be kind to yourself, and be flexible. We don't need a few people doing it perfectly; we need a *lot* of people doing it imperfectly. But also, be open and adaptable. You picked up this book because you want to make a difference, in the world and in your life, but remember: in order to make a difference, we may have to *do* something different. While you certainly don't have to implement every suggestion in this book, don't avoid doing something *different* just because it's challenging. Take some risks, step out of your comfort zone, and expand your horizons.

Don't do nothing because you can't do everything. Do something. Anything.

May this book be your *anything*, and may it provide the scaffolding you need to build a life based on compassion, creating a ripple effect that can and will change the world for humankind and animalkind.

As the subtitle suggests, the three areas of this book's focus are zero-waste, plant-based, and cruelty-free. I've alternated these topics throughout and signal them by three distinct icons:

- the universal recycling symbol for zero-waste,
- a leaf for plant-based,
- and a bunny for cruelty-free.

Introduction
Compassion and Connection

Why is compassion the foundation and the frame for a book on sustainability, plant-based eating, and animal protection? It's because, whether we care about preventing cruelty to animals, avoiding environmental disasters, or optimizing our health, compassion is the answer. But compassion isn't simply a soft, fuzzy beacon of hope. It is the very catalyst for change. At a time when hopelessness about the future, anxiety over the state of the planet, and cynicism toward one another threaten to undermine our collective and personal well-being, compassion is exactly what's needed in response. Compassion is the solution, but it's a solution many don't look to because of how profoundly misunderstood it is.

If ever a human quality needed a public relations boost, it's compassion.

Simply speaking, compassion is the awareness of others' suffering and the desire to alleviate it. More profoundly, it is a guiding principle in all the world's religions and in most secular philosophies and has been for millennia. It is one of the great human virtues, and yet many people struggle to manifest compassion in their daily lives, regarding it as impossibly lofty—achievable only by saints and sages who possess exceptional levels of purity or piety. Dismissed as naive, sentimental, even saccharine, compassion is often seen as an impractical response to serious matters, incompatible with the evolutionary principle that says only the most ruthless survive in this world that favors cruelty over mercy.

While it's true that compassionate teachings do indeed underscore empathy, kindness, and concern for others, compassion is anything but weak. It requires strength, courage, resolve, resilience, and a deep understanding of another's experience—i.e., empathy. Compassion is anything but passive. It is resolute. It is dynamic. By definition, compassion demands *action*.

I think that one of the reasons compassion is characterized as weak stems from fundamental misinterpretations of Charles Darwin's theory of evolution, the idea that it's a dog-eat-dog world. Every man for himself. Eat or be eaten. Darwin's work, especially his theory of natural selection, indeed acknowledges the competitive aspect of survival in the natural world, where organisms compete for limited resources. But his theory also emphasizes the importance of cooperation, sympathy, and compassion in advancing both individual and species survival.

In 1871, Charles Darwin published *The Descent of Man, and Selection in Relation to Sex*, in which he explores the origins of human behavior and the similarities between humans and other animals. In a chapter called "Comparison of the Mental Powers of Man and the Lower Animals," Darwin describes the genesis of empathy and compassion, exploring how both human and nonhuman animals come to the aid of those in need and how natural selection favored the evolution of this sympathy, this compassion. He argued that communities that demonstrated more compassion fared better than those that showed less concern for others:

> In however complex a manner this feeling may have originated, as it is one of high importance to all those animals which aid and defend one another, it will have been increased through natural selection; for those communities, which included the greatest number of the most sympathetic members, would flourish best, and rear the greatest number of offspring.[1]

What Darwin was talking about here was more than mere physical strength or competition. He was acknowledging that the fittest individuals—i.e., those most likely to survive and reproduce—possess cooperative and social traits that contribute to the success of the group.

Unfortunately, Darwin's nuanced perspective became distorted with the idea of "social Darwinism," a term coined years later and not by Darwin, and a term predicated on the fallacy that societal progress occurs only through fierce competition, with the strongest (read: most superior) rising to dominance and the weakest (read: most inferior) being subjugated by them—a false narrative that stands in stark contradiction to Darwin's actual findings.

At worst, this ideology has been used to justify supremacist and racist beliefs, genocide, ethnic cleansing, eugenics, and other related atrocities. At best, it has succeeded in associating compassion with weakness, naiveté, and gullibility, leaving an individual ill-equipped to navigate the rigors of mortal existence and destined to be devoured by the ruthless currents of modern life.

To be clear, the challenges we face in this world didn't come about because we have so much compassion that we don't know what to do with it. The problems we face in this world come about because we're not living according to our own values of compassion, kindness, and wellness, because we're not reflecting our own ethics in our behavior. It's one thing to say that we're against violence, cruelty, environmental degradation, and perpetual ill health. Most people are. It's quite another to manifest our principles of compassion, kindness, and wellness in our daily actions.

If I had to whittle down *compassion* into one (other) word, it would be *connection*. Compassion is about seeing ourselves connected to—not separate from—other people, other beings, and the universe itself. As waves are to the ocean, we are intricately and inherently interconnected with one another and the rest of creation. When we recognize and internalize this interdependence, when compassion is the lens through which we see the world and our relationship to it, we are naturally compelled to act in ways that cause the least amount of harm—to anyone, including ourselves.

There's a passage in the *Tao Te Ching* that beautifully captures this idea:

> See the world as yourself.
> Have faith in the way things are.
> Love the world as yourself;
> then you can care for all things.

And a similar one attributed to the Buddha:

> See yourself in others. . . .
> Then what harm can you do; whom can you hurt?

And Roman emperor and Stoic philosopher Marcus Aurelius wrote,

> What injures the hive, injures the bee.

Any harm to the collective community also harms the individual members, and vice versa. Any benefit to the collective community also benefits the individual members. There is no way to separate the two, just as there is no way to separate heat from fire.

If compassion is about connection, then its opposite is about separation, and it would be a mistake to think that the opposite of compassion is cruelty. Cruelty is the effect; apathy is the cause. When we see ourselves as separate, when we don't see our interconnectedness, we lack the emotional resonance to both recognize and respond to the needs of others, to the needs of the planet, and even to our own needs. Apathy begets inaction. Compassion inspires action.

While *compassion* tends to be used interchangeably with *sympathy* and *empathy*, compassion is not just about feeling someone else's suffering. By definition, compassion necessitates a commitment to alleviating the suffering of others through *action*.

And action is what this book is all about, which is why I have framed this book around compassion. Our desire to live sustainably, prevent animal suffering, and achieve optimal wellness is contingent upon the presence of compassion. And through this lens, we can aspire to live zero-waste, plant-based, and cruelty-free.

Zero-Waste

Motivated by the desire to reduce pollution, prevent resource depletion, mitigate human-caused climate change, conserve water, eliminate greenhouse-gas emissions, or stop the destruction of essential ecosystems and wild habitats, many people are looking for ways to live more sustainably, consciously, and environmentally friendly.

Zero waste—an old concept with renewed popularity—is a way of thinking and living that addresses all of these concerns, focusing on waste prevention from cradle to grave, not just on waste diversion. From a practical perspective, the goal is to move to a circular economy where no trash is sent to landfills, incinerators, or the ocean. From a philosophical perspective, the goal is to make conscious decisions about what we buy, how we eat, and what we do in order to minimize harm and maximize flourishing.

When most people think of "zero waste," most likely what comes to mind are social media influencers with unrelatable, picture-perfect accounts of their zero-waste triumphs. Luckily, many YouTubers and Instagrammers have moved away from the trend of showing how they can fit five years' worth of garbage into a single mason jar, but it's an image that remains emblematic of the zero-waste movement. No wonder many feel it is an impractical and impossible way to live.

Zero waste is not just about making DIY swaps or reducing packaging. It's a larger ethic, a mindset, a lens through which to see the world, our relationship to it, and our responsibility for it. To be sure, the *zero* in zero waste is aspirational rather than actual. It's about progress rather than perfection.

Plant-Based

Banning single-use plastics, reusing glass jars, and reducing our personal garbage output are all necessary and noble endeavors, but if we truly want to protect natural resources, decrease rising carbon emissions, decelerate biodiversity loss, end deforestation, and eliminate pollution, we need also to omit or substantially reduce our consumption of animal-based meat, dairy, and eggs.

Of course, abstaining from meat, dairy, and eggs is also a way to reflect compassion for ourselves and our loved ones. Whole books and countless peer-reviewed studies have made the case that eating a plant-based diet is the most beneficial, compassionate thing we can do for our health.

Centering our diet on vegetables, fruits, beans, lentils, grains, mushrooms, herbs, and spices means taking in an abundance of vitamins, minerals, fiber, and antioxidants, which promote overall well-being and reduce the risk of cardiovascular disease, diabetes, and certain types of cancer. Additionally, plant-based diets tend to be lower in saturated fat and cholesterol, leading to better cardiovascular health and weight management.

Optimal wellness is the goal. Eating plants and not animals is an effective and pleasurable way to achieve that goal.

Cruelty-Free

As I mentioned in the preface, living compassionately isn't just about eliminating meat, dairy, and eggs. It's also about seeing animals as fellow Earthlings with whom we share this planet. This involves shifting from a perception and relationship with animals rooted in anthropocentrism, dominionism, and exploitation to one of cohabitation, consideration, and awe. Practically, this means everything from helping injured animals, fostering homeless animals, and providing habitats for wildlife to seeking alternatives to animal-based entertainment, animal-tested products, and animal-derived clothing. We'll explore the most effective and enjoyable ways to do this throughout the book.

I'm often asked if I think we really can make a difference in this world, and my answer is no. I do not believe we *can* make a difference. I believe we *do* make a difference.

Every product we buy, every item we eat, every dollar we spend, everything we do has an impact on something or someone else. We don't get to decide whether we *can* make a difference. We get to decide only if the difference we inevitably make is negative or positive. That's it. There are no neutral actions.

That has been an empowering orientation rather than a paralyzing one. There are many things we can do to make a positive difference and to at least mitigate our negative impact. May this book be a guide for you to increase your positive impacts and mitigate your negative ones.

Conduct a Personal Waste and Consumption Audit

In the coming chapters we're going to talk about the benefits of and ideas for creating less waste and consuming more plants, but let's first establish where we *are* before we get to where we're *going*.

- The average person in the United States generates 4.9 pounds of solid waste per day, but most of us underestimate how much garbage we actually create.[1]
- The average American consumes approximately 225 pounds of meat from land animals, 20.5 gallons of liquid cow's milk, and 40 pounds of cheese per year.[2] And yet most people say, "I don't really eat a lot of meat, dairy, and eggs."

The truth is we have no idea how much waste we create or how many animal products we eat until we stop. We don't know how much we do of anything until we stop doing it.

Spending this week paying attention to and recording the physical waste we generate and the meat, dairy, and eggs we consume will be helpful ways to accurately assess our habits—in order to change them. After all, we can't manage what we don't measure.

- A *waste audit* simply means examining and documenting each item we discard during a specific time frame to give us perspective on the volume of trash we generate.
- A *consumption audit* simply means documenting what we eat each day to gain a clearer understanding of our current eating habits, paving the way for informed decisions about our diet.

All you need is a notebook and a pen to record your findings—or an online document you can easily edit. Here's how it works.

WASTE: We need to *know* what we *throw!*

Every time you reach for the trash can to throw something away, whether at home or out and about, write it down. For each recurring item, add a tally mark. It might look something like this:

Empty toilet paper roll ||
Food scrap ‖‖|||
Disposable coffee cup |||
Plastic water or juice bottle |||
Aluminum soda or beer can ||
Pet food can ‖‖ ||
Take-out container ||
Plastic shipping envelope ||
And so on.

At the end of the week, organize your list by the frequency of tally marks. This isn't essential, but I think it provides a helpful visual. I also suggest creating a column that indicates the *category* of waste, or rather what category you *think* the item belongs to. (See below for category ideas.) The goal of the exercise is to identify items that might be diverted from ending up in a landfill, even if we think that's not where they'll wind up.

Categories may vary depending on where you live; for instance, my city offers curbside pickup for kitchen scraps and yard waste, so tissue paper and cardboard can go in either our compost bin (because they break down) or our recycling bin (if they're clean and suitable for recycling). Here are some general categories for you to use as a guide:

Recyclables: paper, cardboard, metals, glass, some plastics
Organics: food waste, yard waste, paper, cardboard
Hazardous Waste: batteries, electronics, paint, chemicals
Landfill Waste: broken items, damaged toys, pens, markers, toothbrushes, used tissues, rubber bands, Styrofoam, disposable razors, electronics, cat litter, dog waste, nonrecyclable plastics

This requires rigorous honesty and the discipline to resist the temptation to *wish-cycle.* "Wish-cycling" is the practice of placing items in the recycling bin that we *hope* are recyclable, even though we *know* they're not or we aren't sure, such as plastic bags, Styrofoam cups, multilayer plastic food packaging, greasy pizza boxes, cling film, and everything else we're tempted to throw into the recycling bin even though it won't necessarily be recycled.

Analyze Your Waste

At the end of the week, examine your list.

- Did you accurately identify items that your city accepts as recycling—such as paper, glass, metal, plastic bottles? (Check local guidelines to see which plastics your municipality recycles.)
- Did you trash items that may *not* be recycled by your city—such as electronics, computers, old or damaged furniture—but that *could* be upcycled, refurbished, or repaired by a third party?
- Did you trash items that could be reused, such as glass bottles or jars, old T-shirts, or aluminum foil?
- Did you throw away things that might have been donated, such as pet supplies, school supplies, books, or toys?
- Did you dispose of hazardous materials (batteries, paint, and chemicals) properly?
- How much organic waste (garden cuttings / yard trimmings, food scraps, leftovers) went into the trash that could have been composted, eaten, frozen, or properly stored in the fridge?
- How many items did you throw away that a local seamstress, cobbler, or upholsterer might have been able to repair?
- How many items were those that were "designed for discard," such as disposable diapers, disposable cutlery, or party decorations such as balloons or streamers?

Identify Opportunities for Improvement

Based on your findings, identify areas where you might be able to reduce waste. For instance, you might try to:

- Make simple swaps for common waste items.
  - › Use Q-tips with paper bases—instead of plastic ones—that can be thrown into the compost.
  - › Try toothpaste tablets instead of standard plastic toothpaste tubes.
  - › Buy soap bars instead of liquid soap packaged in plastic bottles.

- Avoid single-use disposable items.
  › Carry a reusable water bottle everywhere. Most tap water in the United States and other economically developed countries is perfectly potable, so you can fill up wherever you go.
  › Bring your own reusable coffee cup to coffee shops.
  › Use reusable dish towels instead of disposable paper towels.
  › Consider menstrual cups, cloth pads, or reusable period underwear as more sustainable alternatives to disposable tampons and pads.
- Reduce food waste.
  › Repurpose leftovers.
  › Compost food scraps.
  › Freeze or eat what's about to go bad.
  › See Weeks 13 (Declutter Your Fridge), 22 (Play the Dating Game: Understanding Sell-by Dates), and 25 (Your Fridge Is Not a Compost Bin: Eat Leftovers) for more.
- Give away something that someone else might use.
  › Find groups online (Buy Nothing Project, Freecycle, Facebook Marketplace) to gift items you no longer need or want but that someone else does.
  › Identify organizations that will properly recycle, upcycle, or use what you cannot, such as Terracycle, Ridwell, or Habitat for Humanity.
  › Participate in trade-in programs for electronics, smartphones, and computers to prevent e-waste. Apple, Best Buy, Amazon, and Dell all have trade-in programs.

The idea is not to feel overwhelmed, hopeless, or guilty. You will never get to *zero*. There will always be unavoidable trash. The idea is to recognize your habits so you can avoid creating garbage in the first place—when possible and practical. Be compassionate with yourself, but don't do nothing because you can't do everything.

MEAT, DAIRY, AND EGGS: You don't know how much you eat until you stop

For one week, keep a detailed record of everything you eat, including meals, snacks, and beverages. Add a tally mark for each recurring item. For instance:

Scrambled eggs ||
Toast ||
Coffee with cow's milk ||||
Banana ||
Lettuce |||
Carrots ||||
Bell peppers ||
Turkey sandwich |
Chinese take-out |
Ice cream |||
Hamburger |
Pizza with pepperoni |
And so on.

Just as you did for your waste audit, consider ordering them by frequency of consumption and categorizing them (Fruit, Vegetables, Meat, Dairy Products, Grains, Legumes, Chips, Candy, etc.) to give you a fuller picture of how much and how often you eat what.

Don't judge. Just observe.

Identify Opportunities for Improvement

As you go through your week's audit, identify where you can switch out animal products for plants. I don't just mean switching out a hamburger for a salad or swapping out a commercial, store-bought animal product with a commercial, store-bought plant-based product. I mean identify the sensation and satisfaction you get with the familiar animal products you've been eating, and see where you can get the same satisfaction from plant-based versions.

For instance, when we reach for a beef-based burger, it's not because we're "craving" animal flesh. Humans are not obligate carnivores and do not "crave" the meat of other animals. But what satisfaction we do get from that beef-based burger (or any other food) comes from

- fat;
- salt;
- texture;
- flavor;
- familiarity.

And all of these experiences can be met with plants. So, identify what you find satisfying about your favorite animal-based meals—"*salty* bacon," "*creamy* ice cream," "*chewy* meat"—then see if you can meet that satisfaction with plants (or plant-based products). Here are some ideas:

FAT

Fat tastes good, and plant fats are healthy. So, eat the nutrient-rich fats from plants:
- Instead of dairy-based Parmesan, toast walnuts or pine nuts along with a little salt, and pulse in the food processor. Sprinkle over pasta or on salad.
- Blend peanut or almond butter into a fruit smoothie.
- Add nuts and/or seeds to oatmeal or a salad.
- Add avocado, guacamole, or nondairy sour cream to a burrito, fajita, or chili.
- Cook, roast, or grill vegetables with a little oil. Though it's true that some plant fats are saturated, they're molecularly different from that of animal-based saturated fat and do not have the same negative effects on our body.
- Use eggless mayonnaise to make your favorite salad or sandwich (or whatever you'd typically use egg-based mayonnaise for).
- Snack on some olives, or add them to a salad.
- Make a peanut butter and jelly sandwich!

SALT

Most of the sodium in people's diets comes from animal products, so you're doing your blood pressure a huge favor by getting these things out of your diet. Of course, there is naturally occurring sodium in plants, but one thing I can guarantee is that you start to crave salt less after you remove the bulk of it from your palate. Here are ways to bring a salty flavor to your dishes:
- Table Salt: Sprinkle a pinch of salt over dishes just before serving to enhance flavor. Salt flakes are a game changer.
- Smoked Salt: Use smoked salt to season grilled or roasted vegetables, mushrooms, or tofu for a unique and savory flavor profile.
- Soy Sauce, Shoyu, and Tamari: Add to stir-fries, marinades, or sauces.
- Miso Paste: Incorporate into soups, dressings, or marinades for a salty and umami-rich flavor.
- Olives: Chop or slice olives and add them to salads, pasta dishes, or pizzas for a salty and briny taste.

- Pickles: Use pickles or pickle juice to add acidity and saltiness to sandwiches, salads, or dressings.
- Capers: Sprinkle capers over salads, pasta dishes, or roasted vegetables for a burst of salty and tangy flavor.
- Nutritional Yeast: Sprinkle over popcorn, roasted vegetables, or pasta dishes for a cheesy taste.
- Dried Seaweed: Crumble dried seaweed or nori over rice bowls, soups, or salads to add a salty and oceanic taste.
- Plant-based Cheese: Incorporate salty, plant-based cheeses like feta, Parmesan, or blue cheese into salads, pasta dishes, or sandwiches for added flavor.

TEXTURE

Consider the texture you're "craving" and go from there.

Crispy or Crunchy:
- Roast or bake vegetables at high temperatures.
- Use a light coating of oil and seasonings to vegetables, and cook in an air fryer.
- Fry or bake thinly sliced tofu or tempeh until golden brown.
- Make homemade veggie chips by baking (or air frying) thinly sliced vegetables like beets, sweet potatoes, or carrots.
- Toast nuts, seeds, or coconut flakes in a dry skillet or oven.

Chewy:
- Marinate and grill or bake portobello mushrooms for sandwiches or burgers.
- Use seitan, tofu, and tempeh in stir-fries or sandwiches.
- Freeze and thaw tofu before cooking to achieve a chewier texture. (You can freeze a block of tofu for up to 6 months, but make sure to thaw it and squeeze out all the water first. Crumbled, it's perfect for chili or pasta sauce.)
- Cook grains like farro, barley, or brown rice until al dente to add to salads or grain bowls.
- Incorporate cooked beans or lentils into soups, stews, or salads.

Creamy:
- Blend ripe avocados into sauces, dips, or dressings.

- Use coconut milk or coconut cream in curries, soups, or desserts for an indulgent texture.
- Mash cooked beans or lentils to create a creamy base for spreads, dips, or fillings.
- Blend potatoes into soups to thicken and add a creamy texture.
- Blend silken tofu into smoothies, puddings, and mousses.
- Make creamy sauces or dressings using soaked and blended cashews as a base.
- Use hummus for dips and as a sandwich spread.
- Prepare macaroni and cheese or nachos with plant-based cheeses, or make a cheesy sauce with potatoes and carrots. (This will blow your mind. Search online for recipes.)

FLAVOR

Think of all the things you've used to flavor meat: ketchup, mustard, barbecue sauce, Worcestershire sauce, steak sauce, relish, vinegars, oils, horseradish, hot sauce, chutneys, jellies, jams, salsa, soy sauce, wasabi, curries, tahini, pickles, garlic, ginger, onions, lemons, limes, and an endless array of spices and herbs. The flavor is in the plant foods, as evidenced by all the condiments in your kitchen. Use them!

FAMILIARITY

Some of our attachment to certain dishes comes simply from our familiarity with them. This is exactly why food scientists are tasked with creating plant-based versions of animal-based foods. They're known quantities. In other words, some of our satisfaction comes from simply recognizing the *form* of a food—regardless of what the dish is comprised of.

- A sandwich with veggie turkey slices, tomatoes, lettuce, avocado, and eggless mayo ticks all the boxes.
- You won't know the difference if you load up your plant-based burger with lettuce, tomato, avocado, pickles, and other favorite condiments and stick it on your favorite bun.
- Same goes for veggie hot dogs with relish and mustard; chili or tomato sauce made with veggie crumbles; or a milkshake with plant-based milk, chocolate sauce, and sprinkles!

You get the idea.

As for some specific swaps:

Consider Plant-Based Proteins. As we'll discuss in Week 23: Build Muscle. Don't Eat It., protein is prevalent in all grains, legumes, and vegetables (and even some fruits), but some plant foods have higher amounts than others.

- Swap out animal-based chicken in a stir-fry with tofu, plant-based chicken, or more veggies.
- Try a new plant-based product like veggie chicken nuggets.
- Use brown lentils or beans instead of ground beef in tacos or chili. (As I mentioned above, tofu that has been frozen, thawed, and squeezed of all its water makes for a chewy texture that is perfect for tacos, chili, and tomato sauces that call for ground beef.)
- Grill portobello mushrooms as a meaty alternative for burgers or sandwiches.
- Experiment with tempeh bacon or coconut bacon as a flavorful addition to salads or sandwiches. (Bacon is all about fat, salt, and smokiness! In a plant-based bacon, you get the fat from some healthy, plant-based oil, salt from tamari soy sauce, and smoke from liquid smoke. All the flavor. None of the harm.)

Swap Out the Dairy. If ice cream and dairy products were prevalent on your audit, consider plant-based versions instead.
- Try decadent nondairy ice creams made from coconut milk, almond milk, or cashew milk. A variety of brands are available
- Purchase a barista-style nondairy oat creamer for your coffee.
- Use nutritional yeast or toasted pine nuts with salt as a topping for popcorn, pasta dishes, or roasted vegetables.
- Make creamy sauces and dressings using cashew cheese or almond milk.
- Enjoy a dairy-free yogurt parfait with layers of nondairy yogurt, fresh fruit, and granola.

Think about Alternatives to Chicken Eggs. What to use in place of eggs differs according to the role the eggs typically play. (See Week 17: Bake Better without Animal Products.)
- Substitute applesauce or mashed bananas for eggs in baking recipes like muffins, pancakes, or quick breads.

- Mix ground flaxseeds or chia seeds with water to create a gel-like mixture as an egg replacement in baked goods.
- Make a tofu or polenta scramble seasoned with turmeric, onions, and peppers.
- Use eggless mayo or mashed avocado as a creamy binder in dishes like eggless salads (using tofu instead of chicken's eggs).

Because our lives and habits may change from week to week or month to month, you might want to conduct these audits every six months or so to see where there's room for improvement.

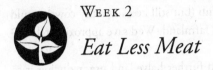

WEEK 2

Eat Less Meat

From the animals' perspective, the ideal amount of meat to consume is *zero*.

From an environmental perspective, there *are* different impacts among different types of meat, depending on whether we're measuring greenhouse-gas emissions, land use, soil depletion, water consumption, or water contamination. Here's what we know.

Whatever the barometer, meat and dairy have a *significantly* higher environmental impact than *any* plant food, whether it be almonds, apples, beans, or blueberries. It must be said that although almonds have been unfairly targeted as being a greater environmental threat than beef, the truth is that their impact is significantly lower, especially when it comes to greenhouse-gas emissions. To illustrate this, the emissions from the highest-impact almond producers are about 2.4 kg carbon dioxide (CO_2) equivalents per 100 grams of protein, while beef averages 35 kg CO_2 equivalents per 100 grams of protein, making beef several times more carbon-intensive than almonds.

That's just comparing *two* items; in general, the meta-analyses and large-scale studies measuring total greenhouse-gas emissions in every stage of production across several food categories consistently find that emissions from plant-based products are as much as ten to fifty times lower than animal-based products. The research is clear: we *must* reduce our consumption of animal products for the preservation of the planet.

The hard truth is, while eating 100 percent plant-based will substantially improve your health, heal our Earth, and prevent violence against animals, the environmental benefits of *everyone* eating *less* meat are far greater than a small percentage of people becoming vegan. To be clear, if the world population shifted to a 100 percent plant-based diet, the benefits would be incalculable. The problem is, I just don't see that happening.

However, if only *half* the population went meat-free only *two days a week*, we would cut greenhouse-gas emissions, land use, and water use by a considerable amount. Just looking at land use, researchers mapped out scenarios of how things would look if everyone in the world adopted different diets.

- Simply cutting out beef and lamb (but still keeping dairy cows) would nearly *halve* our need for global farmland. We'd save approximately 4.9 billion acres.[3]
- Eliminating dairy as well would further halve land use, reducing it to just over 2.4 billion acres.[4]
- If the entire population transitioned to a vegan diet, we could reduce agricultural land use by 75 percent, preserving an area the size of North America, *plus* Brazil.[5]

As an animal advocate, I can't personally advocate switching out beef and lamb (the most environmentally taxing) for chicken and fish, but on an environmental spectrum ranging from good to better to best, that would certainly be the place to start. And there are so many ways we can just *reduce* our consumption of meat, whatever animal it comes from.

1. **Commit to Meatless Mondays.** Consciously dedicating one day a week to plant-based meals is a great start.
2. **Challenge Yourself.** Consider participating in short-term challenges where you commit to a vegetarian or vegan diet for a specified period. This helps you explore diverse plant-based recipes and discover new favorites. (See Week 14: Take a 30-Day Vegan Challenge.)
3. **Gradually Reduce.** Start by substituting one or two animal-meat-based meals per week with plant-based meals.
4. **Know Your "Why?"** Understanding the consequences of our habits can reinforce our commitment. Read books, watch documentaries, or listen to podcasts about the impacts of meat consumption on the animals, your health, and the environment.
5. **Keep Things Familiar.** Identify meals you're already eating that are plant-based (peanut butter and jelly sandwiches, pasta primavera, minestrone, bean burritos, or pasta with marinara sauce), and continue rotating them in your repertoire.
6. **Try New Options at Old Restaurants.** In the spirit of keeping things familiar, continue patronizing your favorite restaurants, but order some plant-based menu items you've never tried before. Or modify what you typically order by making it plant-based—for example, oat instead of cow creamer for your coffee, marinara pizza instead of Margherita, pasta with Arrabbiata sauce instead of Bolognese, etc.

7. **"Plantify" the Recipes You Love.** You don't have to create an entirely new meal repertoire! Take a look at your audit from Week 1, and pick out three or four of your favorite animal-based dishes. Now think of ways to "plantify" them by swapping ingredients or simplifying recipes. For instance:

   Chili: If you typically add ground beef to chili, replace the beef with kidney beans, tofu, or a plant-based meat crumble.

   Spaghetti and Meat Sauce / Meatballs: Replace meat sauce with lentils, mushrooms, crumbled tofu, beans, or plant-based meatballs. Or just enjoy a simple, authentic Italian pasta sauce without any meat at all.

   Pizza: The marinara pizza dates back centuries, originally consumed by sailors and workers because of its affordability and because the natural citric acid in tomato sauce acted as a preservative, allowing mariners (hence the word *marinara*) to bring it along on long voyages. The point is that while you can add nondairy cheese to any pizza, pizza marinara is a classic, consisting simply of a thin crust topped with tomato sauce, garlic, oregano, and olive oil. No need for any kind of cheese at all. (In Italy, marinara pizza is on most menus; in the United States, you'll need to ask for it or say "no cheese.")

   Tacos: Replace the animal meat with seasoned and sautéed mushrooms, black beans, crumbled spicy tofu, jackfruit, or Mexican-spiced plant-based crumbles. Top with salsa, guacamole, and other favorite toppings.

   Burgers: Replace beef burgers with any number of plant-based versions. There are countless recipes in cookbooks or online for making your own from beans, grains, veggies, or mushrooms, but there are also a number of delicious plant-based burgers available at grocery stores everywhere. And every one of them has a lower environmental footprint than any animal-based meat.

   Stir-Fry: Make delicious Asian-inspired stir-fries with just vegetables, or add tofu, tempeh, seitan, or store-bought plant-based meats for added protein, flavor, texture, and nutrition.

   BBQ: Grill barbecue-seasoned portobello mushrooms for a hearty sandwich or main dish.

8. **Commit to Learning Three New Recipes!** With everything suggested above, plus finding three *new* recipes, your plant-based repertoire adds up to well over a dozen! Buy a new cookbook, take a virtual or in-person cooking class, and/or find recipes online.

Of course, over time, it's a good idea to rotate these dozen dishes and not scapegoat veganism if you get bored with what's in your rotation. Getting stuck in food ruts is not unique to and certainly not the fault of *being vegan*. Whether you're vegan or not, everyone gets mired in meal monotony, usually because of lack of motivation and inspiration. While it's fine to rotate your favorite, familiar dishes, just be sure to explore the wide variety of plant-based foods out there to keep your meals exciting and fresh.

Remember, every step you take, every change you make brings you closer to the goals you want to achieve—for animals, for the planet, and for yourself.

Be Prepared to Help Sick, Injured, or Lost Animals

If you've ever encountered dogs who are lost, cats who are homeless, or wildlife who are injured, your instinct to help may have been tempered by uncertainty, fear, or just an aversion to being inconvenienced. Is it safe to approach? Will they respond aggressively? What if I make things worse? What am I supposed to do? Where am I supposed to take them? How long is this going to take?

Torn between empathy and doubt, it's natural to want to walk away, believing that someone else will intervene, but when I've faced this dilemma myself (and I have many times, usually while in a rush to or from somewhere else), always gnawing at the back of my mind is the question: if this isn't *my* problem, then whose is it? Being prepared to intervene starts with *expecting* to encounter an animal who might need my help and being pleasantly relieved when I'm wrong. Basically, I've come to accept that whatever plans I have on any given day (especially if I'm in a rush) may be curtailed by an unexpected critter who happens to cross my path. But a few moments of inconvenience for me can make a world of difference for them.

So, start there: buffer in some extra time when heading out for an appointment or even for a walk. The chances of encountering an animal in need are low, but if it does happen, at least you won't feel as much pressure as you would otherwise. Now that we're prepared *mentally*, let's explore some options for safely, responsibly, and conveniently offering assistance to a domestic or wild animal who may be lost, injured, or in danger.

Have Provisions on Hand

Expect the best, prepare for the worst. One of the reasons we tend to feel stressed in such a situation is because we aren't equipped with the essentials needed to intervene. While we may never need to use these resources, it's better to be safe than sorry.

- Keep leashes, treats, towels, thick gloves, and blankets in your car.
- Keep a flattened cardboard box (large enough for a small mammal) in your garage or trunk.

21

- Have these numbers stored in your mobile phone:
  › your local municipal animal shelter (often called "animal control");
  › the nearest wildlife rescue organization; some have round-the-clock hotlines;
  › a 24-hour emergency veterinary clinic;
  › the shelter and wildlife organizations of your destination when you're going out of town.

Add their addresses, as well. That way, if you are unable to connect to Wi-Fi, at least you'll have the address in your phone and won't need to delay.

Take Direct Action

If you see an injured animal on the side of the road, if it is safe to do so, approach slowly with caution. Injured animals may be scared and defensive, so proceed with care. This is where having gloves and a towel or blanket in your car will come in handy.

Always use gloves when handling an injured animal. Carefully place the animal in a towel-lined box, and transport them to a local animal shelter, veterinary clinic, or wildlife rehabilitation center. Sometimes it's best to call first to make sure they are open or can see you.

Keep in mind that wild animals are just that: *wild*. They experience stress in the presence of humans, so touching them or talking to them—even in a soft, soothing voice—may create discomfort rather than ease. Create a noise-free environment, and resist the urge to pet them.

Provide Temporary Housing

Not all shelters are open 24/7, so if a stray dog or cat you've been able to secure isn't injured and doesn't need emergency care, take them home to give them temporary shelter until the facility is open.

- Keep them separate from your own animals, and give them water, food, and a warm place to sleep.
- For injured wildlife, try to create a safe and quiet space by minimizing noise and disturbance until you can bring them to a professional wildlife rehabilitator. (Call a 24-hour wildlife hotline if you're unsure what to do.)
- For dogs and cats, take photos and create a "found pet" flyer to post around the area where the animal was found and at pet stores and veterinary

hospitals. Also, share on websites such as Petfinder.com and neighborhood groups like Nextdoor.com.

- Let the appropriate animal agencies (SPCAs, shelters, veterinary offices) know you have found a companion animal. Provide a description, or email them a photo in case the animal guardian contacts them.
- As soon as you can, have the animal scanned for a microchip.
- If no one claims a lost dog, cat, or other companion animal, consider fostering them to take the burden off of what is most likely an already overtaxed municipal shelter. (See Week 18: Provide Temporary Housing: Foster Animals)

If you think an animal (or *your* animal) has ingested a poisonous or toxic substance, call the ASPCA Animal Poison Control Center (888) 426-4435 (open 24 hours a day, 365 days a year). Keep this number in your phone as well.

These small steps reap huge rewards, namely feeling prepared; reuniting animals with their people; providing shelter to lost, scared, or abandoned animals; and possibly even inspiring others to step up the next time they're in the same situation.

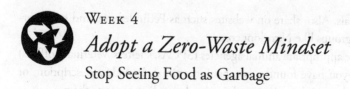

Adopt a Zero-Waste Mindset

Stop Seeing Food as Garbage

Of the edible food Americans buy and bring home, about 40 percent gets thrown in the garbage.[6] While farms, grocery stores, restaurants, and manufacturers create their fair share of wasted food, residential households are responsible for the largest portion: an estimated 76 billion pounds or $240 billion worth of food thrown away annually.[7]

That translates to between $1,365 and $2,275 per household per year.[8]

Dollars aren't the only thing we squander when we waste food; we also waste all of the energy and resources it took to grow, harvest, transport, and package it. Every head of lettuce, basket of strawberries, or leftover risotto tossed into the garbage means wasted labor, wasted time, wasted calories, wasted nutrients, wasted fossil fuels, wasted land, wasted fertilizer, and wasted water.

While most of us don't want to think about garbage dumps, the fact is that food rotting in landfills is a huge environmental problem whose solution must be addressed at all levels—by governments, farmers, restaurants, manufacturers, retailers, and corporations, but individuals as well have a significant role to play in reducing the amount of food thrown into dumps.

The first step doesn't even require a change in our behavior. It requires a change in our thinking. When we stop treating food as garbage in our homes, the benefits are manifold, tangible, and, in some cases, immediate:

- we save money;
- we cook more creatively;
- we deter opportunistic critters who seek sustenance in our discarded food;
- we eliminate odors.

The only reason our garbage cans smell foul is because of all the food we throw away. If organic matter weren't putrefying (rather than properly composting), garbage cans—and garbage dumps—wouldn't stink. With no rotting food in the kitchen waste can, there's no smelly, stinky garbage.

Even if you can't eliminate food waste 100 percent, *reducing* it is essential and doable, especially since we know very well how to mitigate it in our homes. According to experts and extensive studies, the top causes of food waste in our homes are:

- misunderstanding "sell by" or "eat before" dates on packaged foods;
- storing food improperly;
- being unwilling to consume leftovers or produce past its peak;
- buying more than we need;
- taking larger servings than we can eat and leaving unfinished food on our plates.[9]

The good news is that most of our activities that cause food waste can be resolved by making some simple changes in food planning, food shopping, and food storing, all of which are addressed in subsequent chapters.

But before we look at the changes we need to make in our *behavior*, it's worth looking at the changes we need to make in our *thinking*—namely, the need to adopt a *zero-waste mindset* that frames ourselves as *owners taking responsibility* rather than as *consumers merely taking*.

In aspiring to waste less food, the zero-waste concepts of *responsibility*, *value*, *use*, and *ownership* can guide and empower us. The definition of waste that resonates most with me is:

WASTE: Any item for which its owner has stopped taking responsibility.

When viewed through such a lens, even a banana peel isn't *waste*—not until we relinquish our responsibility for it. For instance, once I peel a banana and eat the delicious fleshy interior, the remaining skin is only garbage once I throw it away in a landfill-destined bin for someone else to take care of. However, if I dispose of it so it can be used or collected as "green waste," it's now potential compost.*

In other words, *food scraps* only become *food waste* once we stop taking responsibility for them.

And remember, organic material doesn't just decompose by way of divine intervention. In order for microbes to do their job, certain conditions need to be met: they need oxygen, moisture, the right ratio of nutrients (specifically carbon

---

* Banana skins are actually edible, and some people eat them. You can search online for recipes.

and nitrogen), and they need the dispersal of these nutrients (by way of turning or stirring).

These are *not* the conditions of municipal dumps and landfills. When food is piled up with waste on top of it, there is no oxygen, there is no dispersal of nutrients. As a result, when food is entombed in oxygen-deprived landfills, it generates methane, a greenhouse gas twenty-three times more potent than carbon dioxide in trapping heat within our atmosphere. In fact, solid-waste landfills are one of the largest human-made sources of methane gas in the United States (next to raising livestock and extracting and burning fossil fuels).[10]

As I will reiterate many times throughout this book, the *zero* aspect of zero waste is aspirational rather than 100 percent possible, but when it comes to food waste, I can confidently say that by implementing the suggestions throughout this chapter and subsequent chapters, it really is possible to have a zero *food waste* household. It starts with changing our *mind* about food:

- shifting from viewing food as infinitely abundant and disposable to recognizing it as a precious and essential resource;
- understanding the environmental, social, and economic consequences of food waste;
- challenging the concept that convenience should always come first;
- shifting our focus from *quantity* to *quality* in food consumption;
- cultivating empathy by appreciating the effort that goes into bringing food to the table;
- orienting to gratitude each time we eat.

"Saying grace" before a meal is one way to change our thinking about the meal we are about to eat. It doesn't have to be anything formal—just taking a moment to acknowledge the resources, time, labor, and love that have gone into planting, growing, and harvesting your food and expressing gratitude for these processes and people can go a long way in orienting toward a zero-waste mindset.

Just shifting our *thinking* can reshape our relationship with food and promote a more responsible and mindful approach to consumption and waste. But of course, we also need to shift our *behavior*, and suggestions for that abound in the coming chapters.

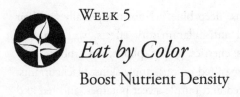

WEEK 5

Eat by Color

Boost Nutrient Density

My message for eating compassionately is simple: *make choices that reflect your values of compassion and kindness.*

My message for eating healthfully is equally simple: *eat by color.*

By doing so, you ensure an intake of diverse vitamins, minerals, and anti-oxidants without getting bogged down in diet fads or by conflicting nutritional advice.

The color compounds in plants form thousands of pigments, and they don't exist merely for aesthetic purposes. Bolstering a plant's defense against insects and diseases, *phytochemicals* or *phytonutrients* (*phyto* is Greek for "plant") also protect plants from environmental stressors such as excessive exposure to UV radiation and free radicals.

And when humans incorporate these phytonutrient-rich plants into their diets, they, too, benefit from these compounds, which offer antioxidant, anti-inflammatory, anti-cancer, and cardiovascular advantages. On the macro level, phytonutrients strengthen the immune system, create healthy blood sugar levels, slow the aging process, and keep the brain functioning optimally. On the molecular level, phytochemicals play vital roles including:

- helping to prevent cell damage;
- inhibiting cancer cell replication;
- decreasing cholesterol levels;
- causing the self-destruction of cancer cells.

It is estimated that there are hundreds of phytochemicals in each of the plant foods we eat, but we can detect the highest *concentration*—the highest *saturation*—of these phytonutrients because of the *color* of the plants. Here are a few to memorize for your next cocktail party conversation:

- Anthocyanins are plant pigments responsible for blue, purple, and red colors in various fruits, vegetables, and flowers. (*Anthos* means "flower" in Greek, and *kyanos* means "deep blue.") Known especially for their antioxidant properties and anti-inflammatory effects, you can find anthocyanins in blueberries, cherries, grapes, plums, red cabbage, eggplant, red and purple potatoes, red onions, apple skins, blackcurrants, purple carrots, black rice, red and purple sweet potatoes, and red and purple (edible) flowers such as pansies, petunias, and violas.

- Beta-carotene is a plant pigment responsible for vibrant orange and yellow hues in numerous fruits and vegetables, including carrots, sweet potatoes, butternut squash, pumpkins, apricots, cantaloupes, and mangoes. An important antioxidant, it is known to boost the immune system, promote skin health, and support vision health. Beta-carotene is a precursor to vitamin A, a nutrient so crucial for eyesight that the chemical name for vitamin A—*retinol*—was coined after the *retina*, the portion of our eye that enables us to see.

- Lutein, another essential carotenoid that concentrates itself in the eye, works with zeaxanthin to prevent such diseases as cataracts and age-related macular degeneration, the leading cause of blindness in people over fifty. Lutein is concentrated in foods that are visibly yellow (*luteus* is Latin for "yellow"), such as corn, yellow squash, yellow bell peppers, and mangoes, as well as in leafy greens such as spinach, kale, collard greens, and Swiss chard. Lutein's bioavailability is improved when cooked and consumed with dietary fats, so don't hesitate to sauté those veggies in some olive oil or roast them and toss in a handful of nuts.

- Lycopene is the reason tomatoes are red and watermelon, grapefruit, guava, and papaya are pink. Lycopene concentrates itself in certain organs of the body, primarily in the lungs and the prostate gland, and a number of studies show promising results using lycopene for prostate cancer treatment and prevention, as well as for improving cardiovascular health, reducing the risk of breast cancer, and preventing macular degeneration and cataracts.

As with lutein, lycopene becomes more bioavailable when consumed with dietary fats after cooking. Pairing lycopene-rich foods with healthy fats, such as olive oil, enhances its absorption by the body. Additionally, cooking and processing tomatoes, such as making tomato sauce or tomato paste, can break down the cell walls of the plant and release lycopene, making it easier for our bodies to absorb and utilize this valuable nutrient.

The list goes on and on—literally! More than ten thousand different phytochemicals have been identified, and researchers are continually discovering more.[11]

While choosing foods by color, don't forget to use your other senses as well. Phytochemicals can also be detected by smell or aroma. For example:

- Allicin is the reason garlic smells so pungent when it's crushed or chopped and is known for its antibacterial and anti-inflammatory properties.
- Curcumin is a compound found in turmeric, known for its powerful anti-inflammatory and antioxidant effects. It's used in cooking and traditional medicine and studied for potential health benefits, including reducing inflammation and fighting diseases like arthritis and cancer. To increase your absorption of curcumin add a pinch of black pepper.
- Limonene, a phytonutrient with antioxidant and anti-inflammatory properties, is found in the peels of citrus fruits like lemons, oranges, and limes.
- Eugenol is a compound found in cloves and is responsible for their strong, spicy aroma. It's used as a flavoring agent in many dishes and has potential anti-inflammatory and analgesic (pain-relieving) properties.
- Vanillin is the compound responsible for the characteristic vanilla scent and flavor. It's found in vanilla beans and is widely used in the food industry as a flavoring agent.

And remember: there are no naturally occurring phytochemicals in meat, fish, dairy, or eggs. *Phyto*, after all, means "plant." It's only when animals eat plants that they take in these and other nutrients. So, skip the middle animal! When we skip the middle animal, we take in all the healthful substances and avoid the unnecessary and unhealthful animal-based saturated fat, lactose, and dietary cholesterol, all of which work against the benefits of the fiber, phytochemicals, vitamins, minerals, and antioxidants prevalent and inherent in plants.

By letting color be our guide, we also rather effortlessly choose whole rather than processed foods. By painting our diets with a rainbow palette of plant foods, we are guaranteed to be eating the most nutrient-rich, flavor-dense, aesthetically pleasing, humane diet possible.

WEEK 6

Keep Flowers . . . Not Bees

We have all heard about the decline of bee populations around the world, which is not good for these pollinators, the plants they pollinate, and the animals (including humans) who rely on these plants for food. In response to what sounds like dire news, many people take up beekeeping as a way to boost the bees!

Well-intentioned though it may be, keeping honeybees and managing beehives does nothing to protect the wild pollinators. Scientists who study bees say it's like farming chickens to save wild birds.[12] Part of the problem is that when we think about bees, we tend to think only of the European honeybee, a species that has been domesticated for crop pollination and honey production and which is not native to the United States. What we should be thinking about are the more than twenty thousand bee species globally, many of which are actually being displaced by the presence of nonnative honeybees.[13]

We cultivate honeybees just like we cultivate chickens, cows, and pigs, and—like all of these nonnative domesticated animals used by the animal agricultural industry—the burgeoning honeybee population does harm to native wild populations. They compete directly for nectar and pollen, they transmit diseases, and they push wild bees out of their native areas.

In addition to habitat loss, another primary reason that wild bees are on the decline is a lack of flowers—so if you want to help bees, forget about beekeeping. Rather, create bee *habitats*.

- Grow pollinator-friendly plants, even if all you have room for are potted plants. You don't need a huge plot of land in order to attract pollinators.
- If you don't have a plot of your own, work with neighbors, local bee conservation societies, and your city council members to create pollinator-friendly public spaces, parks, and road verges.
- Fill your garden or pots with a variety of native flowering plants that are rich in pollen and nectar. Avoid ornamental hybrids that have been bred to produce little or no nectar. Ask your local nursery for recommendations.

30

- Include a variety of flowering species with different colors, shapes, and sizes to provide food throughout the growing season and to attract a wide range of pollinators.
- Avoid neonicotinoid-class pesticides and herbicides, which have been shown to be harmful to pollinators and beneficial insects.[14] If you must use pesticides, choose less harmful alternatives such as Bacillus thuringiensis (Bt), diatomaceous earth, and insecticidal soaps.
- Incorporate some natural pest-control methods like companion planting or by introducing and encouraging the presence of beneficial insects.
- Plant wildflower meadows. Grow native, pesticide-free wildflowers to create safe foraging and nesting areas for pollinators year-round.
- Install beehouses or bee hotels. Build or buy bee hotels for solitary native bees. Place them in sunny, sheltered spots to encourage nesting in the spring, and plant native flowers nearby.
- Create nesting places by keeping some parts of your yard natural and untamed. With the exception of honeybees, which live in hives, most native bee species are ground-dwelling, laying their eggs in tunnels in the ground or in dead branches or fallen logs.
- If you have a lawn, consider replacing it with a pollen-rich flower garden, or at least let it grow some "weeds" such as dandelion and clover.
- Think beyond flowers and shrubs, and plant *trees*, whose blooms provide nectar and whose natural cavities provide shelter.
- Limit light pollution. Reduce outdoor lighting at night, as it can disorient nocturnal pollinators such as moths.
- Don't forget to provide water. Fill a birdbath or tray with water and large pebbles to allow bees to safely drink without drowning. Rinse and refill every few days. See Week 9 for more.
- Advocate for pollinator protection. Support policies and initiatives that promote the protection of pollinators, including bans on harmful pesticides such as neonicotinoids, glyphosate, and organophosphates.
- Buy produce from farms that encourage biodiversity by growing a variety of crops and providing natural habitats for birds and beneficial insects.

By focusing on habitat-creation and flower-planting, we are also helping more than just native bees. A whole range of beneficial insects thrive under such circumstances, including the pollinators, the predators, and the parasitoids, fancy-sounding categories that comprise some of our most familiar garden visitors, such as ladybugs (lady beetles), lacewings, hoverflies, ground beetles, praying mantises, predatory stink bugs, dragonflies, green lacewings, and so many more.

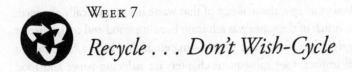

Recycle . . . Don't Wish-Cycle

There is evidence that the concept of recycling—i.e., converting "waste" materials into new materials and objects—has been around since Plato was philosophizing in Ancient Greece, but as a way for municipalities to deal with the garbage crisis of the 1960s and '70s, "recycling" was truly a revolutionary concept.

The problem is that this revolutionary concept focused on garbage as the *problem to be solved* rather than on the product design, materials, and manufacturing *as the source of the problem.* As a result, ordinary citizens got bamboozled into believing that recycling is the solution to all the waste we create.

What's more, the profit-driven industries that create the nonreusables influenced policy enough to ensure that the onus was (and continues to be) on the consumer—not on the manufacturer—to determine what is recyclable, how to properly dispose of items, and whether or not recycling facilities are available or suitable.

Before I embarked on my zero-waste journey, I trusted that if I put an item in the recycling bin, it would be recycled, especially if it had a recycling symbol on it. I soon learned the term for that: "wish-cycling," whereby well-meaning individuals put items into recycling bins, hoping they are recyclable—even when they don't know for sure that they are accepted by local recycling programs.

And that adds up to a lot of waste that goes straight to dumps. In the United States, it's estimated that only about 21 percent of recyclable materials placed in recycling bins are actually captured and recycled, while the remaining 79 percent ends up in landfills. This gap is often due to factors like contamination, insufficient recycling infrastructure, and a lack of public understanding about proper recycling practices.[15]

While the recycling rate for materials like paper and cardboard can reach as high as 68 percent, other materials such as plastic have much lower recycling rates, with only about 9 percent being successfully recycled.[16]

The difference in what we recycle and what ends up in landfills becomes even more striking when we consider how waste has evolved over the past century. Although the amount of garbage we produce today is roughly the same as it was a hundred years ago, the makeup of that waste has dramatically changed. A century ago, much of the waste was ash from burning wood and coal, whereas today, it's largely paper, food, and plastic—materials that have a far different environmental impact. (See subsequent chapters on reducing paper and food waste.)

As for plastic: unlike glass and aluminum, plastic cannot be perpetually recycled without losing its integrity, and so even for those plastic items that may very well be recycled, it's more accurate to say they are "downcycled," meaning that the materials are recycled into a product of lower quality and lower value, such as plastic bottles that are reprocessed to make plastic benches that will eventually wind up in a dump.

While innovators work on more environmentally friendly materials for products and legislators work on making manufacturers accountable—such as in a recently passed California law that bans misleading recycling labels—we individuals can at least do our part to reduce the amount of nonrecyclables going into our waste stream. We can:

1. Adopt a mindset that sees ourselves as *owners* taking responsibility rather than as *consumers* just *taking*—a perspective that can guide our purchasing decisions in the first place.
2. Learn which materials are accepted for recycling in our area and understand the recycling guidelines provided by our local waste-management facility.
3. Rinse containers and remove any food residue or contaminants before recycling them. Dirty items can contaminate an entire truckload of potential recyclables, thus making them destined for the landfill rather than the recycling plant.
4. Keep items like hoses, wires, and cords out of the recycling bin. Since they can get tangled in recycling equipment and cause damage, the entire batch of "recyclables" may wind up being diverted to a landfill instead.
5. Stick to reliably accepted materials such as glass, paper, and cardboard, and avoid placing known nonrecyclable items in the recycling bin.
6. Reduce our consumption of single-use items and opt for reusable alternatives. Reusing items helps minimize waste and conserves resources.

If your city doesn't offer recycling services, consider signing up for a subscription-based recycling program. The oldest and most far-reaching is a company called TerraCycle. Operating globally, TerraCycle functions by partnering with individuals, businesses, and brands to collect and recycle hard-to-recycle materials.

They offer various recycling programs tailored to specific waste streams, such as snack wrappers, beauty products, or office supplies. Participants can sign up for these programs and collect the designated items, which are then shipped to TerraCycle for processing. The collected waste is sorted, cleaned, and recycled into new products or materials, diverting it from landfills and incineration.

Businesses also volunteer to serve as drop-off locations for certain items. For instance, my husband and I both wear contact lenses and thus accumulate empty blister packs that aren't recycled at our municipality's recycling center. Various local optometrists have volunteered to serve as drop-off locations for these empty packs (as well as for the already-worn, discarded contact lenses themselves), which we bring to them and which they send on to TerraCycle to be properly managed.

At TerraCycle, you can find similar programs for prescription bottles, cosmetics packaging, pet food packaging, and so many more types of items that typically wind up in a landfill, since municipalities tend not to recycle such items. While some categories exact a small fee, a number of them are sponsored by manufacturers and thus free to consumers. It's worth checking out to see what's available near you.

In addition to TerraCycle, it's worth mentioning Ridwell, a grassroots, family-owned company that's gaining traction in select cities. While Ridwell isn't as far-reaching as TerraCycle, it offers incredible convenience (home pickup) for those living in the areas it serves, and it's expanding all the time. Ridwell partners with households to collect hard-to-recycle items, such as multilayer plastics (like chip bags and candy wrappers) and plastic film (such as grocery bags and bubble wrap), making it easy to recycle materials that are often difficult to dispose of responsibly.

Recycling *can* and *should* be a tool in our arsenal to combat waste, but a zero-waste mindset sees it as the *last resort* rather than as the *first response*.

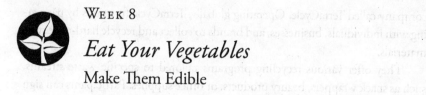

Eat Your Vegetables
Make Them Edible

We've known for decades that a high consumption of vegetables is lifesaving and disease-preventing. If we've heard it once, we've heard a million times: Eat Your Vegetables!

From the day we moved on to solid foods until we moved out of the house, we heard this daily culinary command from our parents. Yet at some point, most of us tuned it out.

Despite dietary guidelines recommending a regular consumption of fruits and vegetables, studies consistently show that a significant portion of the American population falls short. The latest Dietary Guidelines for Americans—developed jointly by the US Department of Agriculture (USDA) and the US Department of Health and Human Services (HHS)—recommend that adults aim to eat 1.5 to 2 cups of fruits and 2 to 3 cups of vegetables every day. According to the Centers for Disease Control and Prevention, which tracks dietary habits, only one adult in ten meets either recommendation.

So, why are we ignoring the most consistent message of our childhood? I have a few ideas.

First, most of us were raised on a meat-centered diet, where vegetables played a minor role and often came from a can, were boiled to death, or were drowning in dairy-based cream sauces and butter. It's no wonder that we didn't get hooked on veggies. It's no wonder that so few of us know what to do with a head of broccoli or a bunch of kale to make it delicious.

Next, we are fierce creatures of habit. Many of us rotate the same dishes over and over, and as the researchers discovered, most people demonstrate very little diversity when choosing vegetables. Here's a secret: when I switched to a plant-based diet, I actually found *more* options. With meat, dairy, and eggs out of the way, a world of plant foods opened up.

Finally, a common barrier that hinders people from reaching the minimum intake of fruits and veggies is the time it takes—or the time they *anticipate* it will take—to chop vegetables.

Change Your Mind

So, before I delve into some ideas for changing our *behavior* to make the cooking process more enjoyable, I want to make an argument first for changing our *minds* about how much time we think is reasonable to spend in the kitchen preparing our meals, particularly dinner. (Most breakfasts and lunches are quick affairs.)

Even for someone who likes to cook, I don't relish spending more than thirty minutes prepping for a meal, unless it's a holiday or special occasion. I can chop vegetables pretty quickly, so often I can do it in less time, but even thirty minutes each day is a perfectly reasonable amount of time to spend making healthful food for our families and for ourselves. After all, *if we don't have time to be sick (and who does?), then we have to make time to be healthy.*

But truthfully, I think we *do* have the time; we just don't always make the *effort.* If we have time to watch cat videos on Instagram or car crashes on TikTok, we have time to chop some vegetables.

Change Your Behavior

There are so many ways to incorporate more plant foods into our rotation; we're hindered only by our imagination and will.

1. Retrain your palate to appreciate the flavors of the vegetables themselves. You don't need more than a little garlic, some fresh herbs, some dried spices, and a little salt to make vegetables shine.
2. Keep vegetables visible, chopped up, and easily accessible in the fridge. Don't keep pushing them to the back of the refrigerator.
3. Reach for (already chopped) raw veggies as snacks instead of potato chips. In fact, don't keep potato chips in the house, especially if they regularly displace plant foods you would otherwise eat.
4. When food-shopping, spend more time in the produce aisle.
5. Try a new vegetable each week.
6. Buy a steamer basket.
7. Shoot for a pound of raw and a pound of cooked vegetables every day; even if you fall short, you'll be way ahead of the curve.
8. Eat the rainbow. (See Week 5: Eat by Color.)
9. Add a serving of veggies to every meal every day—yes, even to breakfast!
10. Try different preparation methods (roasting, grilling, sautéing, steaming, air frying).

11. Make nutrient-dense, plant-based dips like hummus, baba ghanoush, and muhammara. Not only are they healthful in and of themselves, they serve as delicious inspiration for eating more vegetables.
12. Make vegetable-based soups and stews. Add beans.
13. Make fruit smoothies. Add veggies.
14. Serve vegetables *first* so you get full on them first before eating less-nutrient-dense items. This will increase your nutrient intake and decrease your calorie consumption.
15. Use vegetables as pizza toppings.
16. Make sandwiches using only vegetables: roasted red peppers, avocado, red onion, fresh tomatoes—with healthy hummus as your spread.
17. Keep flavor boosters on hand, including balsamic vinegar, tamari soy sauce, dried herbs, dried spices, fresh herbs, garlic bulbs, fresh ginger root, lemons. Simple ingredients are all you need for delicious vegetable preparation.
18. Involve family members when choosing and preparing vegetables. (This is especially fun when you're eating by color.)
19. Buy frozen vegetables to have on hand for quick and easy meal preparation. (Frozen vegetables are often flash-frozen at peak freshness, locking in both flavor and nutrients, making them just as nutritious and delicious as fresh!)
20. Take fifteen minutes a day to chop up vegetables to store in the fridge for easy access. Let's dwell on this one for a moment.

Our overdependence on fast food, frozen food, convenience food, and pre-packaged food has distorted our idea of how much time we should spend in the kitchen preparing a meal. The popularity of cookbooks and YouTube cooking shows notwithstanding, many people feel that taking more than five minutes to prepare a meal is much too long. Yes, it's true that chopping vegetables requires more time than heating up a frozen pizza, but is that really the measuring stick we want to use? Let's take a look at how we can get more veggies in our bodies without feeling the burden of it.

If we chop them, we will eat them! The best way to get vegetables into your belly is to transform them into an edible state. If we open the refrigerator and face a head of cauliflower, a bunch of broccoli, and sticks of carrots with their tops still on, most likely they will remain where they are until they begin to decompose. But if instead we open the fridge to see bags and containers full of cauliflower florets, carrot wedges, celery sticks, and chopped-up broccoli, we're more inclined to make a stir-fry, soup, salad, or a healthy snack. Not only will this increase our consumption of nutrient-dense plant foods, it will also reduce food waste.

Grocery stores have figured out our collective aversion to chopping vegetables, so you can find all manner of pre-chopped vegetables in the produce section these days. While they will be less fresh, less flavorful, more expensive, and heavily packaged, if buying pre-chopped vegetables helps you eat more vegetables, then go for it.

And remember, it doesn't have to be all or nothing. We decide all the time if we want to spend our *time* or our *money*, so perhaps during particularly busy weeks you may be willing to spend more *money* on pre-chopped veggies, but when your calendar is lighter, you may be willing to spend a little extra time chopping vegetables at home—and save money and excess packaging in the meantime.

Maximize your time and tools. If a recipe calls for chopping one bell pepper, chop *two* bell peppers. Add *one* to your recipe, add the other to a storage container. Do this every time you're chopping vegetables. You've already got the chopping board and chef's knife out, so just chop more than you need whenever you're cooking, and just store the extras in the fridge for a snack or upcoming meal!

Multitask (in a healthy way). I'm not a proponent of doing too many things at once, but taking fifteen or thirty minutes (or more) to chop some vegetables is the perfect time to either talk on the phone, listen to a podcast, or crank up the tunes and cook to some favorite music.

Make it a family affair. I've been teaching cooking classes for decades, and so many of my students are parents who feel guilty that they never taught their children how to cook. While it might not be optimal to have the little ones underfoot every time you're prepping a meal, studies show that children who are involved in vegetable preparation are more inclined to eat vegetables. Empower them by giving them their own station, their own jobs, and even their own kitchen tools.

Invest in a few essentials. Speaking of tools, I'm convinced one of the reasons some people don't enjoy chopping vegetables is because they don't have the right tools that make it easy and enjoyable. The two most essential items are a good chef's knife and a sturdy cutting board. Ask around for suggestions, or visit a kitchen supply store where you can test out different knives. And don't forget to keep your knives sharp by either taking them to a professional sharpener or by using an at-home sharpening tool.

Create a *mise en place*. That's just French for "setting in place"—having everything in its place. When preparing a meal, it really does help to take everything you need out of the cupboards and refrigerator before you start slicing and dicing and putting it all together. It helps to stay focused and organized, and it's a lot less distracting.

Once you chop vegetables, it's important to store them properly. See Week 50: Prolong Shelf Life for tips and tricks.

WEEK 9

Provide a Wildlife Habitat

The wild animals who live among us are part of our communities. They're residents and contributors—not outsiders, intruders, or pests, which is often how they're characterized. Our assault on them can be viewed as harbingers of our larger environmental destiny. If we can't attend to the animals in our own backyards, the long-term chances for biological diversity in the rest of this world are bleak.

Every animal whose space we share in our neighborhoods—from the diurnal deer, squirrels, bees, and birds to the nocturnal foxes, skunks, rats, raccoons, mountain lions, and opossums—faces challenges that threaten their very survival every day:

- noisy leaf-blowers and unleashed dogs;
- speeding cars and light pollution;
- rampant habitat loss;
- nonnative landscapes they *can't* eat;
- native plants they're hindered from or punished for eating;
- fences that inhibit their ability to travel freely and safely to find food, water, or shelter.

Biological diversity is declining at alarming rates, and since the underlying cause is easy to identify (human behavior), the underlying solutions (human behavior) are equally apparent. A few changes can make all the difference.

Prioritize Native Plants

Plant species that naturally occur in your region have adapted to the local climate, soil, and wildlife, making them an essential part of the local ecosystem. While planting 100 percent native species is *ideal* for maximum ecological benefits, *ideal* isn't always possible. A well-balanced approach would involve *incorporating* native plants as the backbone of your garden and using nonnative plants thoughtfully—with an understanding of their potential impact on local biodiversity. Consult local nurseries and gardeners for lists of native species.

Celebrate Herbivores!

Those of us lucky enough to see deer outside our windows are also aware of the bad rap they get for being overpopulated "pests," destroying and damaging gardens and causing hazardous car accidents. The reality is much more complicated. By hunting and driving away wolves and mountain lions, humans have disrupted the natural balance that keeps deer populations in check.

Using evidence-based strategies, many communities have started moving away from the simplistic and ineffective model of merely killing deer to reduce their numbers and are now implementing more-effective measures such as reintroducing natural predators and using contraceptives for humane population control.

Aside from being prey for predators and food for scavengers, deer serve important ecological roles:

- They contribute to biodiversity by helping to shape plant communities through their grazing habits, which can create habitats for other animals.
- Their movement helps in seed dispersal, which promotes the growth of various plant species.
- They provide recreational, mental, and emotional benefits through wildlife watching and ecotourism activities. Seeing these peaceful grazing animals can evoke feelings of tranquility and awe, connecting us to nature and providing a sense of calm and wonder. When we look through the same lens as we would when seeing gazelles on an African safari, we might have a greater appreciation for the herbivores in our own backyards.

The irony is that we fill our gardens with plants deer love and then vilify them for eating the very things they thrive on! Here are a few ways to coexist peacefully with these beautiful animals:

- Protect new plantings with fencing, repellents, and *wildlife-friendly* netting. (Birds and animals can become entangled in fine mesh and suffer tremendously, so practice prudence when using it as a deterrent.)
- Offer up a few "sacrificial" plants that deer find particularly palatable, deliberately diverting them away from your more valuable plants.
- On that note, taller and heartier trees can withstand a little nibbling, especially once they're more mature. Even if deer eat (or rub on) the lower branches of established trees, the trees themselves are likely to endure.

- Look at thriving neighboring gardens to see what grows despite the presence of deer.

Avoid Harmful Chemicals

Gardening can be deeply rewarding, but it's also where we learn to coexist with nature's imperfections. Try various nontoxic solutions for managing weeds and intruders.

- Hand-pick snails and caterpillars from your leafy greens, and relocate (rather than kill) them. Copper strips also work wonders for deterring snails.
- Gently pull weeds that would compete with your preferred plants, and use mulch to suppress weed growth.
- Maintain healthy soil with proper nutrients and organic matter to improve plant resilience against pests and diseases. (See Week 30: Garden for Good.)

Create Wildlife Corridors

Wildlife corridors, by allowing animals to move freely through fragmented habitats, reduce conflicts with humans and provide safe passages for individuals who are otherwise forced onto dangerous roads to find shelter, food, or water.

- Fences are the biggest hindrance to migrating wildlife, so consider removing or modifying a fence to allow for free movement.
- For smaller animals, install ground-level, one-foot-wide gaps in the fence to allow them to pass through or under.
- When it comes to iron or metal fences, remove decorative spikes at the top that can impale deer if they can't clear the fence. Consider covering up slats and openings that deer—especially young fawns—can get caught in. For instance, I affixed chicken wire to our slatted metal fence low enough so that the deer can't squeeze themselves between the bars but high enough so that the smaller critters (skunks, racoons, opossums, cats) can easily pass through.

Provide Shelter

Install birdhouses, bee hotels, bat boxes, and nesting boxes for birds, bees, and bats to breed, lay eggs, or roost. Leave dead trees or fallen logs as natural habitats for insects, fungi, and cavity-nesting animals.

Avoid Over-Maintenance

Reduce lawn mowing and pruning to allow for the growth of wildflowers and the development of natural cover for wildlife. Leave areas of your yard undisturbed to provide safe spaces for animals to forage and hide.

Provide Water

Install birdbaths, ponds, or small water features to offer a consistent source of clean water for wildlife.

- Attract a variety of animals—from busy bees and sassy hummingbirds to squirrels, crows, raccoons, and skunks—with fountains of different sizes and shallow ceramic/terracotta trays of water on the ground.
- Keep birdbaths high up off the ground so birds feel safe from predators.
- Speaking of predators: place birdbaths near tree branches where birds can quickly seek cover if they sense danger. But ensure there are no hiding spots nearby where predators like cats and hawks can easily ambush the birds. I positioned colorful metal tomato cages next to some of our bird fountains so the birds can alight on them to and from the fountain. They use them all the time.
- Position birdbaths in the sun. Notwithstanding the popularity of cold plunges among humans, birds don't want to bathe in cold water. They want to cleanse themselves in warm(ish) water.
- Also, avoid filling birdbaths to the brim. Birds aren't looking to swim; they bathe by standing in shallow water, lowering themselves, and splashing the water onto their bodies with their wings.
- Place large stones in moving fountains to give young birds something to perch on and prevent them from drowning.
- Ensure that your windows are bird-safe, especially if you're attracting birds with food or water, to prevent collisions. Mark windows with decals to make them visible, keep shades closed during the day when possible, or plant vegetation near windows to break up reflections.

Implementing even some of these ideas will be beneficial for both you and your wild neighbors. You can even get your backyard or garden certified as a humane wildlife habitat through organizations like the National Wildlife Federation.

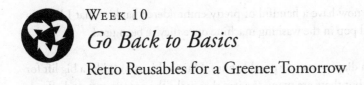

Go Back to Basics

Retro Reusables for a Greener Tomorrow

Humans have a penchant for romanticizing the past, and we do so as quickly as it's transformed from the present. Every generation waxes poetic about "how much better things were in the bygone days," whether those days were in our own lifetimes or several centuries or millennia ago—and whether or not things really were ideal. (They probably weren't.)

Having said that, when it comes to living sustainably, there are *some* aspects of the past worth revisiting. You don't have to turn into a Do-It-Yourselfer or emulate Ma and Pa from *Little House on the Prairie*, but there are some old-school switcheroos we can make that result in having a lighter footprint on the Earth without too much inconvenience.

Choose bars of soap instead of body wash in plastic bottles. Not only will soap bars make you perfectly clean, this simple switch reduces energy consumption during production, minimizes plastic waste destined for landfills, and is most certainly less expensive. Not only are you not paying for bulky packaging, many soap bars are packaged in simple eco-friendly materials like paper.

Choose cloth napkins, sponges, and kitchen towels instead of single-use disposable paper products. According to the Environmental Protection Agency, Americans generate about 3.8 million tons of tissue paper and towel waste each year, with the majority of it ending up in dumps—i.e., not composted or recycled.[17] Counters can be wiped with a sponge, spills can be soaked up with a towel, and mouths and hands can be cleaned with cloth napkins that can be reused indefinitely.

Carry reusable cloth handkerchiefs instead of using disposable tissues. I never thought I would use reusable hankies. I shudder with mild revulsion at my childhood memory of being handed a used handkerchief by my father whenever I needed to blow my nose. But thinking about deforestation, energy and water consumption, and chemical pollution in the production of disposable tissues, I got over it. I now have a handful of pretty embroidered hankies that I keep in my purse and pop in the washing machine once they've been used.

Choose cloth diapers over disposable ones. I know this sounds like a big lift for new parents, but there are many services that make the process easy and affordable. An estimated 4.1 million tons of disposable diapers are generated annually, and of course, by design, they are destined for the dump.

Make some of your own cleaning products (hear me out!). I don't think this has to be done for everything, but making a few cleaning products from scratch will *reduce* the need for plastic bottles. For instance, you can make a simple concoction of vinegar/lemon juice + water for window and glass cleaning and baking soda + essential oils as an abrasive for tubs.

Use metal lunchboxes instead of plastic bags for packed lunches. They are durable and can be used for years.

Choose glass or metal over plastic packaging, when possible. Glass and metal are more easily recyclable and have a lower environmental impact. (See Week 7: Recycle . . . Don't Wish-Cycle.)

Invest in rechargeable batteries instead of disposable ones. This reduces the number of batteries that end up in landfills.

Pay a repair technician to fix household items, electronics, or appliances instead of immediately replacing them. This extends their lifespan and reduces overall waste.

Make your own snacks at home, such as granola bars, trail mix, or popcorn, and store them in reusable containers. This reduces the need for individually wrapped snacks.

We don't have to be rigid, we will never be perfect, and everyone has a different level of tolerance for such things. Some people love the challenge of taking apart broken electronics and finding the faulty gizmo. (I don't.) Some people love sewing. (I don't.) Some people love cooking from scratch. (That's me!) Find what works for you, and enjoy the process.

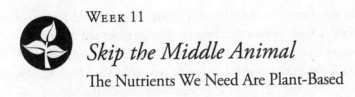

WEEK 11

Skip the Middle Animal
The Nutrients We Need Are Plant-Based

Perhaps the most persistent, disempowering nutrition myth we have been taught is that *the nutrients we need are animal-based.*

We're told we should get calcium from cow's milk, omega-3 fatty acids from salmon, and protein from animal-based meat and eggs—leading to the misconception that to abstain from animal products is to be deficient in essential nutrients.

Nothing could be further from the truth.

Animal flesh and fluids are not the *source* of calcium, omega-3 fatty acids, and other nutrients. They are the *carriers.*

The amount of resources it takes to bring animals into the world only to use them up and kill them is wasteful at best and macabre at worst. By skipping the middle animals and getting our nutrients directly from the source (plants), we substantially reduce resources, demonstrate our compassion for animals, and tread more softly on this Earth.

To illustrate the fact that the nutrients we need are plant-based, let's look at a few nutrients we're commonly told need to be consumed through animal products.

Calcium

Calcium is a mineral found in the ground. We don't mine minerals from animals; we mine minerals from the soil. Just as minerals like calcium, potassium, and magnesium are essential for *plant* growth (see Week 30: Garden for Good), so, too, are they essential for *human* growth.

Cows have calcium in their milk only because they eat plants—theoretically. Actually, the majority of dairy cows in the United States are kept on large-scale industrialized operations where they have limited or no access to pasture. In order to live up to the marketing claim that dairy is a high-calcium product, the industry supplements cows' feed with calcium. [See Week 24: Stop Acting Like a Baby (Cow).]

You could supplement *your* feed with calcium, or you could just make calcium-rich foods a staple in your diet. Putting aside the ethics and the environmental impacts of raising animals just to get to a mineral that's in their milk because of the supplements they're fed, it doesn't even make sense from a nutritional standpoint. Not only do green leafy vegetables contain the highest concentration of calcium among all whole plant foods—with collard greens, kale, bok choy, and beet greens taking the lead—the bioavailability of calcium in these foods is more than twice the amount of what it is in cow's milk. Bioavailability refers to the proportion of nutrients that are absorbed and utilized by the body from a given food source. The bioavailability of calcium from cow's milk is about 30–35 percent. From green leafy vegetables such as kale, broccoli, and bok choy, it's about 50–60 percent.

More than that, these greens are packed with *essential* iron, magnesium, vitamin A, vitamin C, and vitamin K, folate, fiber, antioxidants, and phytochemicals and are devoid of *nonessential* saturated fat, dietary cholesterol, and animal protein.

You can't say that about cow's milk.

Omega-3 Fatty Acids

Another nutrient often associated with animal products is omega-3 fatty acids. Fish are commonly recommended as the primary source of omega-3s, but fish don't naturally produce omega-3 fatty acids; they consume them through their diet. The salmon, mackerel, and sardines—all of the "fatty fish" purported to contain high amounts of omega-3 fats—obtain them from eating algae, phytoplankton, or other animals who feed on aquatic plants.

In other words, these healthy fats are plant-derived.

To increase our omega-3 fatty acid intake without consuming saturated-fat and heavy-metal-laden aquatic animals, we are better off going straight to the source: plants. Flaxseeds, chia seeds, hemp seeds, walnuts, edamame, sea vegetables, and algae—all have high quantities of omega-3 fats.

In addition, many experts suggest that everyone (not just vegans) take docosahexaenoic acid (DHA) supplements for a more convenient, reliable, and consistent source of these essential fats. Unlike food sources that rely on our bodies to convert fats like alpha-linolenic (ALA) and eicosapentaenoic acid (EPA) to DHA, supplements offer pre-converted forms for better absorption. Numerous brands offer algal-based supplements, offering essential nutrients without causing unnecessary harm. (See Week 26: Don't Supplement . . . Complement.)

Protein

Protein is made up of amino acids that are essential for building and repairing cells in the body. There are twenty amino acids that the body uses to create proteins; our body makes eleven of them, and the remaining nine must be obtained through our diet, hence they are *essential*. As we discuss in Week 23: Build Muscle. Don't Eat It., it's true that we need to consume protein, but it's not true that plants don't contain enough. The largest and strongest animals on the planet are herbivores who derive all of their muscle-building protein from the plants they consume. We might take a cue from these mega-herbivores and get our protein directly from plant sources. Lentils, legumes, tofu, quinoa, and nuts provide essential amino acids without the need to go through the middle animal. And if you're looking for a quick dose of healthy additional protein, plant-based protein powders from wholesome sources are also available.

Vitamin B12

Vitamin B12 is the only essential nutrient we need that's not plant-based. But it's not animal-based either. It's synthesized by bacteria. Just as the feed of dairy cows is supplemented with calcium, so, too, is the feed of "beef cattle" supplemented with vitamin B12.

For a reliable and consistent intake of vitamin B12, it's advisable to turn to supplements or fortified foods. These sources provide a controlled and measurable way to ensure adequate B12 levels and prevent deficiency, regardless of your dietary choices. Keep in mind that vitamin deficiencies affect the general population and are not exclusive to vegans.

The bottom line is that it makes absolutely no sense nutritionally, ethically, or ecologically to go through an animal to get to the nutrients that the animal got because the animal (theoretically) ate plants.

When we skip the middle animal, we go straight to the vitamins, minerals, fiber, folate, antioxidants, and phytochemicals that enable us to live and thrive. When we skip the middle animal, we increase the nutrients' bioavailability. When we skip the middle animal, we skip the cruelty, as well as the unnecessary and harmful animal-based saturated fat, dietary cholesterol, lactose, and heavy metals.

Embrace Ethical Entertainment
The Case Against Animal Captivity

On a recent trip to Italy, while touring the baths of Pompeii, a woman in my group looked up at a mosaic illustration of a boy swimming with dolphins and declared that the ancient Romans must have loved animals. I conceded that they most likely regarded some animals with awe and wonder but also reminded her of the grueling chariot races in the Circus Maximus, the gruesome fabricated "hunts" in the Roman Forum, and the egregious animal slaughter that took place in the Colosseum—all for the sake of human pleasure. Many of these animals were also stolen from their wild homes and transported from across the Roman Empire to be used in these deadly spectacles.

The ancient Romans were, like us, a diverse and complicated people. They were resourceful, intelligent, and innovative. They were also violent, ignorant, and opportunistic.

In all these ways—both good and bad—we are the same.

Animal menageries and forced animal performances—precursors to modern zoos and circuses—date back to some of the earliest civilizations, led mostly by the wealthy, ruling elite who maintained private collections of exotic animals as symbols of their power and prestige. Not much has changed—except perhaps in the modern way we shroud the cruelty of animal captivity in the guise of science and conservation, and animal performances in the guise of tradition and culture.

Choose Sanctuaries, Not Zoos

Zoos emphasize their role in educating the public about wildlife, instilling a love of animals, and fostering appreciation for the natural world, though evidence suggests that zoos do not in fact increase our knowledge or understanding of either animals or nature. One of the reasons is because zoo animals don't exhibit natural behaviors in captivity. What they exhibit instead are neurotic behaviors and repetitive rituals, such as pacing, bar-biting, swaying, and circling—no matter how much zoos design their enclosures to mimic their respective natural habitats.

Zoos celebrate their breeding programs as a means to propagate endangered species, but to what end? Not a single lowland gorilla—or for that matter black rhino, elephant, or orangutan, all of whom are classified as critically endangered—has ever gone from a US zoo back into the wild. Zoos populate zoos. Breeding programs replenish cages—not ecosystems.

For captive breeding programs to be successful, wild habitats must be preserved. The dollars spent on animal exhibits would be better spent on protecting already-wild individuals and rapidly disappearing habitats. There are a few examples of this, but not enough. More than that, thousands of animals in zoos—even accredited zoos—are betrayed by their alleged champions every year. To curb overpopulation, animals are killed on a regular basis in zoos around the world either to be fed to other captive animals or to zoo patrons. If they're not killed, "surplus animals"—those individuals whom zoos no longer considered profitable because they're neither young enough nor cute enough to attract crowds—wind up in circuses, in private residences, and even in the hands of taxidermists.

Not only is captivity not beneficial for those who are captive, it instills nothing in us but arrogance, supremacy, and apathy, perpetuating the idea that nonhuman animals are here for us to use, abuse, and exploit for our own pleasures and purposes.

This isn't the case when we admire birds in our backyards; watch bees pollinate flowers; spot wild turkeys, deer, and lizards from a hiking trail; or visit animals who have been rescued from neglect or abuse and brought to sanctuaries.

Whereas zoos are created for the purpose of entertaining people, sanctuaries and refuges are created solely for animals. By definition, zoos and animal theme parks confine animals in enclosures in order to exhibit them to the public. The role of animal sanctuaries, on the other hand, is to provide a safe, permanent home for rescued domestic or previously captive wild animals, free from exploitation and abuse.

And though sanctuaries do not exist for the pleasure of curious humans, many do offer the opportunity for people to work with or spend time with the rescued residents, depending on the type of animal and the stress it may or may not cause individuals or certain species.

Before visiting any type of animal sanctuary or refuge, always do your research first to make sure you're not inadvertently supporting a disreputable, glorified zoo. Sanctuaries dedicated to wild animals can be especially deceptive, as they may misrepresent themselves to attract visitors and money. Look for accreditations, certifications, or endorsements from reputable organizations, and only visit sanctuaries that prioritize animal welfare, conservation, and ethical practices. The best ones may not even allow visitors.

- **Farmed animal sanctuaries.** Domestic animals—pigs, cattle, goats, sheep, chickens, turkeys, donkeys, and horses who would otherwise have met a slaughterhouse fate—fare the best in a sanctuary atmosphere, where they can roam on acres of pastureland. Search online for a farmed animal sanctuary near you.
- **Wildlife rehabilitation centers.** Whether for birds, mammals, or aquatic animals, many facilities around the world focus on rescuing and caring for injured or orphaned wild animals, providing visitors and volunteers with a chance to learn about conservation and witness animal rehabilitation efforts. While the goal for reputable rehabilitation centers is to return the animals back to the wild, some animals deemed unfit for release may remain at the rehab center and serve as ambassadors for their beleaguered species or be relocated to a wildlife sanctuary.
- **Wildlife refuges.** There are a number of credible wildlife preserves around the world devoted to wild animals who, though they will never again have to entertain humans, could never survive in the wild on their own—declawed, defanged, and dependent as they are. Some of them offer opportunities for visitors to see for themselves the individuals whose lives have been spared, whose bodies have healed, and who have become the ambassadors for individuals in similar circumstances who will never be rescued. Even if you can't visit, you can provide support through monetary and in-kind donations.
- **Elephant sanctuaries.** Requiring a lot of space and an experienced, knowledgeable staff, elephant sanctuaries provide rescued and retired elephants with a safe haven free from exploitation and captivity. In Asia, they offer refuge for elephants traumatized by industries like logging and tourism; in the United States and Europe, they provide permanent homes for individuals rescued from zoos and circuses. These sanctuaries offer elephants the chance to live in a natural environment with proper care and dignity, addressing the physical and psychological needs of these majestic animals.
- **Primate sanctuaries.** Depending on the species and their needs, sanctuaries for nonhuman primates serve as havens for individuals rescued from captivity, laboratories, deforestation, zoos, circuses, and the film and television industries. Doing their best to mimic natural habitats, these sanctuaries address the physical and psychological needs of primates, ensuring they live with dignity and peace. Some sanctuaries prioritize the well-being of their residents over public tours, but most likely they offer opportunities for volunteers.

- **Big cat sanctuaries.** Like all wild animals, large cats, such as lions, tigers, leopards, jaguars, and cougars, do not thrive in captivity and find their way to sanctuaries after being rescued from zoos, circuses, or the pet trade. Reputable sanctuaries provide ample space and enrichment, and may limit public engagement.

Sanctuaries serve as crucial havens for animals rescued from exploitation, abuse, and neglect, who slowly begin to heal from physical and psychological trauma, develop relationships with others of their own kind, and become ambassadors for those in similar circumstances who may never be rescued.

However, to truly address the root causes that necessitate sanctuaries, we need to make some changes in our own behaviors:

- eating plants and not animals;
- learning about animals through books and nature documentaries;
- immersing ourselves in nature and observing animals in their natural habitats;
- volunteering with conservation organizations;
- taking up wildlife photography;
- protecting dwindling wild habitats and ecosystems;
- embracing ethical ecotourism both domestically and abroad;
- supporting legislation that prohibits wild animal acts, vivisection, and the wildlife pet trade.

Choose Entertainment, not Exploitation

The practice of using and killing animals for our own pleasure runs throughout history and cultures. It's certainly not unique to the ancient Egyptians or Romans, and it did not end with them. We like to believe that we've shed our barbaric selves, but the violent echoes of the past resound in our own amphitheaters—in horse races, in bullfights, and in the circuses where sentient animals are forced to perform degrading acts for the entertainment of humans.

Animal performances distort the very qualities we admire—their strength, prowess, and intelligence. What we're witnessing instead is a façade born from terror and fear, as animals are coerced into unnatural behaviors through pain and intimidation.

Ethical alternatives to animal circuses abound. Not only do they enable us to connect with and witness the incredible world of animals, they are wonderful ways to teach children to respect and appreciate their magnificence and autonomy.

- **Animal-Free Circuses:** Many circuses have shifted to human-centric acts, acrobatics, and other exciting performances without the use of animals. These spectacles showcase the extraordinary talents of human performers and leave animals alone.
- **Ethical Wildlife Safaris:** View wild animals in their natural habitats—safely and humanely—through responsible ecotourism, nature reserves, or wildlife safaris.
- **Animal-Free Theme Parks:** Many carnivals and amusement parks offer rides, performances, and attractions without the use of animals.
- **Educational Programs:** Attend lectures and workshops that focus on wildlife conservation, ecology, and the importance of coexisting with animals in their natural environments.
- **Animal Documentaries:** Explore the fascinating world of animals through documentaries and films that showcase their natural behaviors and habitats.
- **Volunteer Opportunities:** Consider volunteering at animal shelters, sanctuaries, wildlife rescue centers, or conservation organizations. (See more ideas in Week 49: Volunteer for Animals.)
- **Fundraisers and Adoption Events:** Attend events that promote stewardship and compassion, such as companion animal adoption drives or wildlife conservation fundraisers.
- **Outside Your Windows:** Dozens of wild animals live just outside our windows, whether we live in a city apartment or on acres of land. Just looking out the window can give you a front-row glimpse into the intricate world of wild birds, squirrels, raccoons, skunks, opossums, deer, foxes, coyotes, and more. Observe behavior and relationships, journal about what you see, take photos and videos, and treat your backyard like the wildlife preserve it is.

By opting for these ethical alternatives, we contribute to a collective shift toward a more compassionate and sustainable relationship with the animal kingdom. We can revel in the awe-inspiring attributes of animals while championing their right to live free from exploitation and confinement.

If we changed our thinking about animals from "how do we see them?" to "how do they see themselves?" we would make very different decisions about how we spend our leisure time and disposable income. If we recognized that animals' inherent desire for freedom, life, autonomy, and self-determination is as strong as our own, we would deem it unacceptable to put them behind bars for just being themselves.

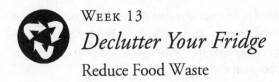

Declutter Your Fridge

Reduce Food Waste

Reducing food waste at home starts with decluttering your fridge. By organizing items strategically, you make it easier to see and access what you already have and also prevent forgotten items from lurking in the back and spoiling. A well-organized fridge helps you keep track of expiring food, utilize leftovers, and plan meals effectively.

Set aside a few hours for this task. If you've never done it before, it will take a little time to *make* it organized, but once you've got a system in place, it will take less time to *keep* it organized.

1. Start by taking *everything* out of your fridge, even those unidentifiable bits hiding in the back of the produce drawers. Properly dispose of expired items.
2. Wipe down *all* the shelves and drawers.
3. Use a "lazy Susan" / turntable (or two) to keep your commonly used ingredients and condiments in sight and to prevent leftovers from getting forgotten about in the back. If you've started this project before buying a lazy Susan, use large plates as placeholders.
4. Alternatively, use clear plastic bins to organize your main shelves. Your refrigerator likely has designated areas like crisper drawers, but you can add more by using these trays and bins, which maintain order and simplify the process of pulling out items when you need them.
5. Arrange your refrigerator based on your cooking and eating habits: keep frequently used items or items you want to finish in easy-to-reach spots, and place ingredients you use less frequently in areas that are a little less accessible.
6. Keep your leftovers organized and well sealed with airtight food storage containers. Use masking tape to label the date and items within.
7. Make sure your refrigerator is set to the optimal temperature to keep food fresh. The recommended temperature is around 37°F (3°C) for the main compartment and 0°F (–18°C) for the freezer.

8. Keep newer items behind older ones to ensure that nothing gets forgotten or expires. This practice helps you use up older items before they spoil.
9. Hang a whiteboard or chalkboard near your fridge/freezer to maintain a list of what needs to be eaten first.

Similarly, when it comes to your freezer, label and date items before storing them in clear containers or bags. Group similar items together, store them properly (in airtight containers), and rotate items regularly in order to use older ones first.

While this may not be the last time you will have to declutter your fridge and freezer, if you keep them organized, it will never take as long as the first time. Check out Week 25: Your Fridge Is Not a Compost Bin: Eat Leftovers for much more about eating leftovers as a means for preventing food from spoiling in the refrigerator and getting freezer burn in the freezer.

WEEK 14

Take a 30-Day Vegan Challenge

In Week 2, I suggested eating *less meat*, which is a great first step for preventing greenhouse-gas emissions, overuse of land and water, and water pollution. But if you want to also curb deforestation, safeguard biodiversity, mitigate climate change, optimize your health, and prevent cruelty to animals, consider eliminating animal products altogether.

If you're ready to give it a try, I suggest committing to it for 30 days. Thirty days are going to pass anyway. Today is the day to begin.

Why 30 Days?

Most experts agree that it takes three to four weeks to change a habit, so taking a 30-Day Vegan Challenge will help to establish new habits, replace old ones, and provide enough time for the body to respond and show improvements. While change is hard—even if that change is for the better—a 30-day commitment is a manageable and achievable way to see tangible results but still short enough to keep you motivated throughout and give you a sense of accomplishment by the end.

Where to Start

1. **Know your "why."** While we probably all care about being healthier, not hurting animals, and having a lighter footprint on this planet, there is usually one door through which we walk when we're motivated to make such a change. Take a little time to get clear about why you want to make some changes. Read some books, listen to some podcasts, watch some documentaries on that topic.
2. **Take a food audit,** as I recommended in Week 1. You simply don't know how much you do of something until you stop doing it, so take a few days before starting this challenge to document how you eat now, what you typically reach for, and what your food triggers are.
3. **Recruit friends and family.** Especially if you live with others or are the main cook in the house, it will make the process so much more enjoyable if you do it together.

4. **Create goals.** Having some specific goals in mind will make the experience even more impactful, but be realistic so you're not disappointed. Even if you want to lose 50 pounds, it won't be reasonable or possible to do so safely in 30 days. Start small. Create achievable goals: "Lose 5 pounds in 30 days." "Learn two new recipes." "Reduce my cholesterol by 20 points in 30 days." (See Week 32: Know Your Numbers.) Those are all realistic and attainable goals.

5. **Identify patterns.** As I keep emphasizing, it's difficult to see the forest for the trees when we're in it. Stepping out of the familiar enables you to identify patterns that have kept you stuck. You might realize that you reach for foods like dairy-based cheese or ice cream during stressful times, or that you "crave" greasy fast food late at night. By removing these options from your diet for 30 days (or choosing plant-based versions of them), you become more mindful of your eating patterns and can develop healthier habits.

6. **Document your experience.** Keeping a daily journal will help you see these patterns, but also gives you a space to celebrate successes.

7. **Get support.** There are numerous resources out there to help you feel less overwhelmed, including my own 30-Day Vegan Challenge book and online program, but whatever you do, connect with others who are on the same journey. Find a community that can provide not only recipes and resources but encouragement, accountability, and inspiration.

8. **Be open and honest.** Accept that you will make mistakes and accidentally eat animal products over the course of the 30 days. Be open to trying new foods, learning new things, and stretching your comfort zones. And while perfection isn't the goal, try to be consistent and resist intentionally "cheating"—not only to show yourself what you're capable of but also to maximize the benefits you will no doubt experience—physically, emotionally, and spiritually.

Over the last several decades, it truly has been an honor to witness thousands of transformations, and people are often surprised that changes can happen so quickly. Committing for 30 days allows you to see these benefits firsthand, which often provide compelling motivation to continue beyond the challenge.

It's just 30 days—not forever, but sometimes that's all it takes to spark a lifetime commitment.

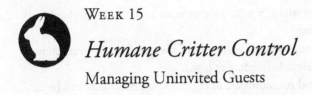

Humane Critter Control
Managing Uninvited Guests

Fears and negative perceptions about wild animals abound. Whether they arise from evolutionary survival instincts or sensational fictional narratives, the result is the same: some animals are valued, while others—especially those who appear uninvited into our homes, like rats, snakes, cockroaches, and bats—are demonized and labeled as "pests" or "vermin." Despite their admirable qualities, these creatures are often cast in a negative light, shaped by both human nature and cultural myths.

We are all inhabitants of this world. We are all inherently interconnected. By shifting our perspective and acknowledging our shared space, we can cultivate harmonious relationships and learn to peacefully cohabitate with other species—even while keeping them from taking up residence in our homes. The animals we call "pests" are typically more afraid of us than we need to be of them, but that doesn't mean they don't seize opportunities to find cozy spots in our homes for shelter and warmth, or a safe place to give birth and raise their young. But keep in mind that their goal is not to terrorize us, but simply to survive.

Assuming, however, that we don't want critters puncturing water pipes (which rats can do), chewing electrical wire (which squirrels can do), weakening the structure of the house (which termites can do), or dying in our attic, we need to stop inviting them in in the first place by closing up their access points: the inevitable cracks, holes, and gaps that form in every human-made structure.

And, while you're sealing up the ways animals can get *in* (professionals can help), it's crucial that you first entice them *out*. Unfortunately, most people resort to lethal traps (glue or snap) and poisoned bait, all of which are cruel, deadly, and unnecessary. Humane eviction should be the first line of defense, and there are several ways to do this:

1. **Identify the type of animal inhabiting your home, and plan accordingly.**
   a. If you hear pitter-patter in the attic during the day, it's most likely squirrels, who sleep at night.

   b. If you hear rustling in your attic or walls at night, it's probably rats making nests.

   c. If you see droppings and evidence of ravaged food in your kitchen, it's most likely mice feeding at night.

   d. Raccoons and opossums are nocturnal foragers, so they will be outside at night—a good time to implement other eviction methods (see below) and close up identified holes.

2. **Create an inhospitable environment.** Most animals dislike loud sounds, bright lights, and noxious smells, all of which can be in your arsenal for both evicting and deterring uninvited house guests. Once they leave, be sure to seal up those entry points to prevent reentry.

   a. Place bright or blinking lights in the attic or crawl space they're inhabiting.

   b. Place ammonia-soaked rags (in ziplock bags with holes poked in them) in the place they've moved into.

   c. Also try natural repellents like citrus, cinnamon, and cayenne pepper.

   d. When it comes to mice, ants, and roaches, it's all about food. Keep your kitchen clean. Don't leave crumbs on the counter, and keep all food in tightly sealed containers.

   e. Similarly, implement the suggestions found throughout this book for avoiding throwing food in the garbage. It's an invitation to opportunistic animals looking for a free meal.

   f. Use caulk and weather stripping to seal all possible entrances, especially during the rainy season.

3. **Install a one-way exclusion door that allows critters to leave but not to reenter.** Seek assistance from wildlife professionals who can assess your situation and install the exclusion device correctly.

4. **Use a live trap.** Live traps, such as the Havahart two-door rat and squirrel trap, offer an ethical and humane solution for capturing animals; it's just a matter of enticing your furry target with food they're attracted to (rats love cheese—including dairy-free cheese!—and squirrels love peanut butter). Once you trap your critters, you need to release them, and doing so just outside your home is the most humane (and legal) thing to do—while you're simultaneously working on sealing up access points to your house.

5. **Avoid killing when possible.** When it comes to the smaller buggers, such as spiders, stink bugs, or caterpillars, I find it pretty easy to urge flying insects toward an open window or door to shoo them out. For

spiders, I just carefully pick them up with a tissue and return them outside. After all, when we can avoid killing, shouldn't we?

6. **Leave some animals to professionals.** Eviction of snakes, bats, and hornets, for example, are best left to those who can remove them safely and humanely.

    However, be wary of "wildlife exclusion specialists" who promise to "humanely relocate" the animals they trap. The majority of the time, they gas or drown wildlife, assuring the compassionate homeowner that they're just relocating them to a pleasant park. Not only is this inhumane, it is most likely illegal—if it happens at all.

In the end, making compassionate decisions about uninvited critters benefits not only the animals but also our own peace of mind. By choosing humane methods, we create harmony in our homes and inspire others to take kind, thoughtful actions in managing wildlife. Together, we can coexist with the creatures who share our spaces.

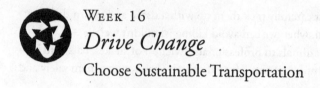

WEEK 16

Drive Change

Choose Sustainable Transportation

The good news is that government regulations, technological advancements, and consumer preferences have collectively led to modern cars being cleaner and more fuel-efficient than ever before. The bad news is that transportation today—everything from cars and trucks to planes and ships—still contributes to approximately 25 percent of the world's carbon dioxide emissions.[18]

So, what's a peripatetic *compassionista* to do? Like so many issues, there's not one answer for everyone. Some of it depends on where you live, how you live, and where you work. Here are some best, better, and good suggestions for sustainable transportation depending on the distance you have to travel and the lengths you're willing to go.

Short to Medium Trips

1. **Best: Walk, Bike, or Take the Train**
- For short to midrange distances, walking and cycling are the most environmentally friendly choices, reducing travel emissions by around 75 percent compared to driving a car.
- Public transportation, particularly trains, follows closely, reducing emissions by around 80 percent for midrange trips.
- Compared to domestic flights, train trips slash emissions by about 86 percent.[19]

2. **Better: Electric and Hybrid Vehicles**
   The good news is the cost of lithium batteries has decreased substantially in recent years, making the cost of electric vehicles and plug-in hybrids a much more affordable—and definitely the most environmentally friendly—choice for personal transportation, emitting significantly less CO_2 than a gasoline-powered car. So, if driving is a necessary part of your life, opt for an electric car, but keep it a reasonable size.

3. **Good: Size Matters + Sharing Is Caring**
- When it comes to gasoline-powered cars, smaller cars remain better for local pollution and human health, and they're also more affordable. The bigger the car, the less fuel-efficient it is and, therefore, the more CO_2 it emits.
- Additionally, many of our cities were designed to accommodate cars from decades ago. Bigger cars—including large electric vehicles—mean bigger driveways, wider streets, more-sprawling parking lots. In other words, large electric trucks and SUVs aren't the answer. The smaller, the better—whether it's a gasoline- or battery-powered vehicle.
- If possible, incorporate car-sharing into your transportation options: it reduces your carbon footprint, saves money, alleviates air pollution, and tackles congestion.

Long-Distance Travel

On one hand, airplanes have become much more efficient in recent years, and by utilizing renewable energies they will most likely continue to improve. On the other hand, airplane emissions are increasing because of growing global demand. Having the data enables us to make informed choices when it comes to long-distance travel.

1. **Best: Embrace Boats and Trains**
   When traveling internationally, if possible, opt for trains or boats over flying.

2. **Better: Consider the Distance When Choosing between Flying or Driving**
   - For trips under 600 miles / 1,000 kilometers, flying has a larger carbon footprint than driving a medium-sized gasoline car the same distance—and even higher compared with driving an electric vehicle.
   - However, for longer journeys over 600 miles / 1,000 kilometers, flying would actually emit fewer greenhouse gases compared to driving alone over the same distance. (There are higher emissions in short flights because a significant amount of energy is used during takeoff.)[20]

3. **Good: Fly Smarter and Fly Less**
   Reduce Plane Travel: When possible, reconsider or reduce air travel, whether for business or pleasure. Professionally, consider conducting

meetings online or over the phone when possible. Personally, consider taking a good old-fashioned road trip. My husband and I have made a goal to sleep in every county in California (there are fifty-eight), and we have just a handful to go. It has inspired us to explore our home state and see things we wouldn't otherwise have seen, and we've been able to do it all without flying. Create a similar goal—drive across the country, visit every national park, hike in every national forest. And of course, if you're able to do this in an electric vehicle or by train, your footprint will be minimal. If you don't own an EV, you can rent one.

Choose Direct Flights: Opting for direct flights and avoiding layovers when possible will reduce the amount of carbon emissions used.

Fly Economy Class: Flying economy class generally has a lower carbon footprint per passenger compared to business or first class.

Offset Carbon Emissions: Consider purchasing carbon offsets to compensate for the emissions produced by your flight. These funds typically go toward projects that reduce carbon emissions elsewhere, such as renewable energy or reforestation initiatives. But do your research to find reputable companies with rigorous certification processes, transparent offset projects, proven track records, and real commitment to environmental integrity and accountability.

Pack Lighter: Pack lightly to reduce the weight of the plane, as lighter planes require less fuel to travel the same distance. Consider taking only a carry-on for your next flight.

Choose More Fuel-Efficient Airlines: Some airlines have more fuel-efficient fleets, use alternative fuels, or have committed to reducing carbon emissions through technological advancements and operational improvements.

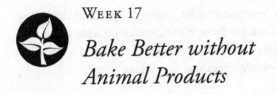

Bake Better without Animal Products

Weeks into your journey of compassion, you may have cut out (or cut down) your consumption of meat, and you might even be in the middle of a 30-Day Vegan Challenge (see Week 14).

Wherever you are at this point, let's look at *why* and *how* to eliminate eggs from your diet—particularly from your baked goods.

Baking with eggs is so ingrained in us that it's hard to separate the two, but let's be clear: chickens did not get together and decide that their eggs would make great binding agents in cakes and cookies. Eggs are an essential part of a bird's reproductive cycle, containing the potential to develop into living chicks (if fertilized), but because we have made them such a significant aspect of cooking and baking, we force hens to produce 92.6 billion eggs annually in the United States alone. That's 308 million hens being exploited for their eggs[21]—the majority of whom are confined in cages with three to ten other birds, where they are unable to perform even basic natural behaviors. Trapped in cramped wire cages, they live their entire lives standing on metal floors that painfully dig into their feet. With no room to spread their wings or even turn around, these birds suffer immense physical and psychological distress, and are denied the freedom to preen, perch, or even flap their wings. Such confinement leads to frustration, injury, and, often, severe behavioral issues from the lack of space and stimulation. Even those in so-called confined housing suffer similar overcrowding where they unable to experience any semblance of a natural life.[22]

Bakers and non-bakers alike suffer from the misconception that baked goods require chicken's eggs, cow's milk, and dairy-based butter. The fact is in order to create delicious, rich, decadent baked goods what you need is moisture, leavening, binding, and fat.

Not to mention texture, flavor, and structure.

Yes, animal products provide these, but so do plant foods—and even better, because plant-derived ingredients are better for us, better for our planet, and better for the animals!

There are many ways to create binding, fat, moisture, leavening, thickening, and even glazing without animal products; it just depends on what you're making. Once you identify the *effects* of the different ingredients called for, you'll be able to confidently and successfully "veganize" any baking recipe.

- Animal's milk is the easiest thing to swap out in recipes that call for milk, opting for almond, soy, oat, cashew, or coconut milk, all of which are commercially available in both sweetened and unsweetened versions— and most of which can be easily made at home. (See Week 38: Cook from Scratch.) Use plant milks in a 1:1 ratio to replace dairy milk in recipes.
- Instead of animal-based butter, opt for plant-based butter. Many non-dairy butters are commercially available and work perfectly well as a 1:1 replacement for dairy-based butter. It's just fat from plants rather than animal fat; it's equally effective but even healthier.
- As for eggs, replacing them is really a matter of what their purpose is in a given recipe. Identify that first and foremost—and consult the table below for guidance. And keep in mind that chicken's eggs are often superfluous and thus can often be left out without even being "substituted." It just depends on the role they're playing.

If an egg is used for...	Fat	Binding	Moisture
Try instead...	Plant-Based Butter Coconut Cream Coconut Milk Coconut Butter Coconut or any Vegetable Oil Mashed Avocado Nut Butters	Agar-Agar Silken Tofu Plant-Based Yogurts Commercial Vegan Eggs Fruit Purée Aquafaba Flax Eggs Chia Eggs	Silken Tofu Plant-Based Milks Plant-Based Yogurts Commercial Vegan Eggs Fruit Purée Aquafaba Flax Eggs Chia Eggs

If an egg is used for...	Leavening	Thickening	Glazing
Try instead...	Baking Powder Baking Soda + Vinegar or Lemon Juice Whipped Aquafaba Baker's Yeast Self-rising Flour Sourdough Starter	Agar-Agar Xanthan Gum Cornstarch Arrowroot Potato Starch Pectin Commercial Vegan Eggs	Plant-Based Milks Maple Syrup Agave Nectar Fruit Jams or Jellies Plant-Based Butter Coconut Oil Aquafaba

When you contemplate baking without eggs and dairy products, you might feel like you have to *re*learn how to bake. And it's true—with anything you're learning, relearning, or trying for the first time, there is indeed a process. There is a learning curve.

But trust me. Once you grasp the fundamentals, new habits replace old habits, and those new habits become second nature.

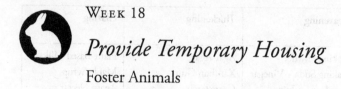

WEEK 18

Provide Temporary Housing
Foster Animals

Several decades ago, I volunteered at an underfunded county animal shelter socializing cats, cleaning their cages, and providing some enrichment to their solitary lives. Adoption days were few and far between, and one day I impulsively decided to bring home a kitten to give her some reprieve from the cage. I wasn't adopting her. I was fostering her.

That's when I became a *foster failure*, not because I adopted her—which is what the term often implies—but because my good intentions turned into a disaster for my own two cats (Simon and Schuster) for all the stress caused by the mere presence of this little cat (Kelly).

Characteristically sensitive and territorial, both Simon and Schuster immediately fell ill and developed crystals in their bladder—preventing them from urinating. Fortunately, after much discomfort and many medical interventions, they recovered—and Kelly was subsequently adopted by a loving family.

While I continued to volunteer for cat rescue groups, I was quite scarred by that traumatic experience and overcorrected, swearing off fostering altogether. Until I decided to try again just a few years ago.

This time, I prepared.

Having learned from the mistakes I made previously, I chose not to integrate my foster cats with my own (now Charlie and Michiko). I gave my fosters their own safe place in their own separate room, leaving my kitties to feel secure and unthreatened.

It was a triumph.

I have now successfully fostered dozens of cats and seen them through to their adoptive homes. And my cats have hardly noticed a thing. (Mostly.)

After years of experience, I can offer some suggestions to make fostering cats—or dogs—a successful and stress-free experience:

1. **Work with an Established Rescue Organization.** A reputable organization that will provide support, guidance, resources, and open

communication throughout the fostering process is essential. They will help match you with the right foster animal and work to place them in a loving forever home once they're ready for adoption. Read the foster agreement carefully, and know what to expect ahead of time.

2. **Prepare Your Home.** Decide in advance where your new arrival will sleep, eat, pee, poop, and play, and get those areas and supplies ready before the animal shows up.

3. **Prepare Your Schedule.** When accommodating the needs of a temporary resident, changes in your regular routine are par for the course. Be open, be flexible, and build in some buffer throughout each day to account for unexpected circumstances.

4. **Gain Household Consensus.** Make sure all members of your household are on board with fostering. Create expectations, discuss responsibilities, and anticipate potential challenges beforehand.

5. **Start Slowly.** Begin by fostering one animal (or a bonded pair) at a time to understand the commitment and adjust to the routine. Because my foster cats have their own separate room from the rest of the house, I always take a bonded pair so they can enjoy each other's company when I'm not in the room with them.

6. **Create a Backup Plan.** Have a plan in place if you have to leave town for an emergency or are going on vacation. Know who to contact if your home is not the right fit for your foster animal and you need an alternative plan.

7. **Practice Self-Care.** Taking care of another living being is a lot of work and can be emotionally and physically demanding. Prevent burnout and ensure a positive fostering experience by prioritizing self-care. Ask for help from friends or family members if you need it.

8. **Be Patient.** Foster animals may have behavioral issues or medical needs that require time and patience to address.

9. **Document Success.** One of the most gratifying aspects of fostering animals is watching them come out of their shell and become more confident, affectionate, or exploratory. Celebrate and document such milestones (in writing, photos, and videos) to remember these triumphs but also to share them with the rescue organization you work with.

10. **Spread the Word.** Share your experience with others to raise awareness about the importance of fostering and to encourage others to get involved.

No doubt about it, when I foster, my workload is doubled—cleaning additional litter boxes, keeping my office door shut so my fosters don't escape, constantly sweeping excess litter from the floor, playing with my fosters several times a day, and making sure my own cats don't feel neglected.

But I think the barrier most people have to fostering—whether it's dogs, cats, or bunnies—is not the practical work but the emotional toll it takes.

After all, how do you remain emotionally unattached enough to let them go when the time comes?

The answer is: I *don't*.

It is, in fact, my emotional attachment that makes me better able to care for my fosters until they find their forever home. Of course I fall in love with all of them—I spend hours a day socializing them, helping them to build confidence, helping them to cultivate resilience—but if I weren't emotionally invested, I wouldn't be as effective.

Like a momma bird who has to nudge her fledglings out of the nest for their own good, my job is to prepare my fosters for their transition to their permanent home. Without fail, I cry every time I say goodbye, and I always need to take some time before I foster again, but that time always comes because of the lives it directly changes.

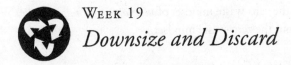

Downsize and Discard

There's a concept in Taoism that runs throughout the ancient text the *Tao Te Ching*; it's the idea of *having* without *possessing*. Of *wanting* without *grasping*. The problem isn't that we *have* things. The problem is that we *cling* to them. The problem is that *they* wind up owning *us*.

When we define ourselves by the things we possess, we have a hard time letting go of them, and we purchase things we don't really need. When we *cling*, when we *grasp*, when we *desire*, when we *possess*, things control *us* rather than the other way around.

I'm embarrassed when I think back on the beginning of my zero-waste journey. I never considered myself to be someone who had a lot of *stuff*. And I think that, relatively speaking, I *didn't* and I *don't*—but when I took inventory, it turned out I certainly had things I wasn't valuing and could easily pass on to someone else who would value them.

Thinking about my death galvanized me.

As a practitioner of Stoicism, thoughts of my mortality are never far from my mind. Central to this philosophy is the concept of *memento mori*—"remember that you must die." It serves as a reminder of the inevitability of death, of the transient nature of life. And so I started thinking that the last thing I want when I die is for someone to be burdened with the task of having to go through all my stuff in order to determine what is valuable and worthy of keeping and what should be discarded.

And so reflecting on my death—or, rather, anticipating it—compelled me to start going through my closets, drawers, crawl spaces, and garage to identify things I don't need and don't use. Aside from the satisfaction of knowing I'm not deferring my responsibility to someone else, decluttering just feels really good.

It's now part of my weekly routine.

Determining what needs to go isn't always easy; knowing what to do next can be equally difficult, which is another reason to do it myself. No one else should be tasked with this responsibility. To help navigate obstacles, determine priorities, and stay on course, I created a list of guiding questions that act as a framework for staying in the zero-waste mindset of *use, value,* and *responsibility.* (See Week 4 for more about the zero-waste mindset.)

- Am I valuing this item? That is to say, am I *using* it?
- Am I *enjoying* this item (and thus *valuing* it)?
- Can I use this item anymore? Do I *need* it? Will I ever need it? Is it something I can borrow from someone else if need be?
- Can someone else *value* it—i.e., *use* it?
- If not, do I need to consult my city or other resources to find out how I can dispose of it in the most *responsible* manner?

Most of the time the answer is: give it away, which then triggers the process of finding the person who wants or needs what I have to give. This is the *responsibility* part of the equation.

In the past, I simply gathered items into a box and brought them to Goodwill. Arriving, I'd feel a pit in my stomach seeing all of the dumpsters filled with items brought by well-intentioned people like me who had the same idea. I walked away feeling that I had just made my stuff someone else's problem. That's not to say Goodwill and similar organizations don't have a place, but I can't say that dumping a bunch of my belongings in a dumpster and never knowing their fate was necessarily taking responsibility.

And so I took a closer look at my options and found that there were better ways of properly rehoming or responsibly discarding the items I no longer wanted or needed:

1. Searching for organizations that need exactly what I have to give. Many organizations have specific wish lists
2. Asking friends, family, and neighbors if they would like particular items
3. Selling items on eBay, Facebook Marketplace, Craigslist, and other online platforms
4. Having a good, old-fashioned garage sale
5. Bringing books to a library or used bookstore
6. Leaving valuables to people in our will
7. Giving things away through networks such as Freecycle or Buy Nothing groups

The last one has been paradigm-shifting for me. The Buy Nothing Project was founded in 2013 to encourage the giving of consumer goods and services to people who want what you have. And because the groups are organized by zip code, you are interacting with people who are essentially neighbors—and potential new friends. Post anything you'd like to give away, ask for anything you'd like to receive or borrow. When someone claims an item you're offering, you know it's going to someone who really wants it, and if they change their mind or it doesn't suit their needs in the end, they regift it back to the group. The generosity I've witnessed has been astounding, and it's a genuinely uplifting experience.

This aspect of the zero-waste journey has been a gift and a liberation.

In addition to decluttering, feeling lighter, and being accountable for things I bought in the first place, I've met new people, connected with more members of my community, and given without wanting anything in return.

It's not to say that belongings of mine won't be left behind after I die, but at least there will be less, and my hope is that what remains will be valued by someone else who treasures it for a time before they, too, let it go.

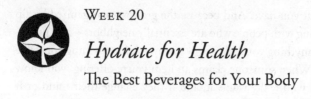

WEEK 20

Hydrate for Health
The Best Beverages for Your Body

Technically speaking, water and breast milk are the only two beverages we have a physiological need for. Everything else is optional. However, just as we aim to optimize our health with nutrient-dense *foods*, we can do the same when it comes to choosing what we drink.

Water

We all know that water plays a crucial role in almost every bodily function—hydrating cells, regulating body temperature, aiding digestion, and supporting vital organs like the kidneys and liver—but does the age-old recommendation of 8 glasses per day still hold water? The short answer is yes, mostly. Based on the best evidence we have to date, health authorities suggest that women should aim to drink 4–7 cups of water per day, and men should aim for around 6–11 cups. This takes into account the rich water content of fruits and vegetables, so be sure to eat a diet rich in both to maintain hydration levels and to absorb essential nutrients and fiber.

Sparkling water offers the same hydration benefits as still water and can be a refreshing alternative if that's your preference. Just be sure it's free from added sugars, artificial sweeteners, and added sodium.

For people who dislike plain water or who are accustomed to artificially flavored or sweetened beverages, infusing (hot or cold) water with herbs, fruits, and flowers can make hydration more enjoyable, and of course infusions impart nutrients as well. For instance, mint and ginger can aid digestion. Basil provides vitamins A, K, and C for immune support. Rosemary adds antioxidants that may enhance circulation and brain function. Citrus fruits provide vitamin C, and hibiscus contains powerful anthocyanins, which can reduce inflammation and support heart health. Lavender and chamomile promote relaxation and sleep. It's also a great way to use fresh herbs and fruits before they spoil.

As for bottled versus tap water, recent studies indicate that bottled water isn't necessarily safer or cleaner than tap water—and of course it creates unnecessary plastic waste and cost—but even if you live in a place with safe drinking water, filters and purifiers are recommended to filter out additional, potentially harmful particles. And whether you install a faucet filter or keep a pitcher with a built-in filter in the fridge, it's important to replace filters regularly according to the recommended dates to optimize filtration and prevent bacterial buildup.

Tea

I have a confession to make that may result in my expulsion from American culture. *I have never had a cup of coffee in my life.* I have been a tea drinker all my life, and my interest in and affection for it borders on obsession. I drink mostly green tea, about four cups a day, and it turns out that my love of it has immeasurable benefits. Green tea, the most extensively studied of all the teas, is linked to reduced risks of several cancers, improved brain function, and protection against neurodegenerative diseases, but oolong, white, and black tea have also been shown to be similarly beneficial, so pick your favorite or mix and match.

Green, white, oolong, and black teas all come from the same plant—the Camellia sinensis, a small evergreen shrub native to East Asia, specifically China and India. What makes these varieties different from one another is their processing and oxidation levels.

- White tea undergoes the least processing and is not oxidized, offering a delicate floral flavor and high antioxidant content.
- Green tea is minimally processed and also not oxidized, retaining a high level of antioxidants.
- Oolong tea is partially oxidized, striking a balance between the flavors and benefits of green and black teas.
- Black tea is fully oxidized, resulting in a stronger flavor and higher caffeine content.

The health benefits of green, black, white, and oolong teas stem from their rich antioxidant content, which helps reduce inflammation and boost heart health. These antioxidants include polyphenols, powerful compounds found in plants that help combat oxidative stress and reduce inflammation, lowering the risk of chronic diseases like heart disease, cancer, and neurodegenerative disorders. While polyphenols are found in most plant foods, their concentrations are highest in berries (blueberries, strawberries, blackberries, raspberries), dark chocolate, nuts and seeds, olives, beans, red wine, tea, and coffee.

Coffee

Despite debates on coffee's effects, numerous peer-reviewed studies show that moderate coffee consumption is also linked to several health benefits. Studies suggest that the caffeine in coffee can enhance cognitive function and improve athletic performance. Additionally, coffee contains antioxidants and other compounds that have been associated with a reduced risk of neurodegenerative diseases like Parkinson's and Alzheimer's. However, excessive intake can lead to anxiety, insomnia, digestive discomfort, and increased heart rates. Caffeine content varies between tea and coffee. On average:

- an 8-ounce cup of coffee contains about 95 mg of caffeine;
- an 8-ounce cup of black tea has roughly 47 mg of caffeine;
- an 8-ounce cup of green tea usually contains 20 to 30 mg of caffeine.

Oolong and white teas have caffeine levels that fall between these ranges.

While both tea and coffee have their health benefits, green tea might have the edge due to its high levels of antioxidants and other beneficial compounds such as L-theanine, which slows the release of caffeine into the bloodstream, moderating its effects. Whereas the caffeine in coffee can lead to jitteriness, tea tends to offer a milder, more sustained stimulation.

As a tea enthusiast, I highly recommend finding a tea purveyor near you or online that can guide you in which loose teas to try, especially if tea-drinking is new for you. Many people are familiar only with bagged teas, which are typically blends of lower-quality black teas that require sugar to make them palatable, or cheap grades of green tea that taste stale or unpleasant.

I recommend looking to China for green teas such as Cloud Mist, Bi Luo Chun, and Dragonwell; Japan for green teas such as Sencha, Matcha, and Gyokuro; Taiwan for oolong teas such as Dong Ding; and India for such black teas as Darjeeling and Assam. China also produces the most delicate white teas, such as Silver Needle and White Peony.

Unlike coffee or black tea, green teas don't call for creamer or milk, which is the next beverage we'll look at.

Plant-Based Milk

Once children are weaned, there's no physiological need for milk of any kind, whether from animals or plants. However, since I know most people will not live by water alone, there's nothing wrong with including plant-based milks in your diet to provide texture, flavor, variety, and nutrients. Like cow's milk, they are often fortified with such nutrients as calcium, vitamin D, and vitamin B12; but unlike cow's milk, they are free of saturated fat, cholesterol, casein, lactose, hormones, and antibiotics, making them a healthier option that supports heart health, digestive comfort, and optimal wellness.

No single plant-based milk stands out as better than another; each has different attributes depending on the brand. They can all be used interchangeably in baking, but if you're a coffee drinker and can't live without cream, coffee aficionados swear by oat creamer as the best choice for steaming and frothing.

Ultimately, water is all we need, but variety is the spice of life, and we have a number of healthful beverage options for tantalizing our taste buds and optimizing our health.

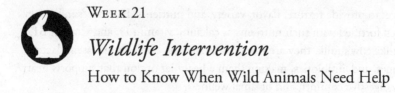

Wildlife Intervention

How to Know When Wild Animals Need Help

Dwelling in my own little wild kingdom has its blessings and challenges. I'm immensely grateful to live in a house where I see (and hear) all manner of deer, skunks, squirrels, opossums, raccoons, foxes, coyotes, rats, mice, turkeys, and several species of birds every single day.

On the other hand, I've also borne witness to my fair share of wounded, sick, or distressed animals—deer with broken legs, coyotes with mange, raccoons with distemper, squirrels with head injuries. Sometimes I've been able to save them. Sometimes not, but I find comfort in the fact that the safe, quiet, non-threatening space I've created is where animals have come to live—and sometimes to die. (See Week 9: Provide a Wildlife Habitat.)

As we discussed in Week 3, being *prepared* to help an animal who is hurt or injured can mean the difference between life or death and relief or suffering, and having some supplies and provisions on hand for an unexpected emergency can alleviate some pressure from an already stressful situation. But being prepared also means knowing *if* and *when* our intervention is needed at all; sometimes it can cause more harm than good.

Let's explore some common scenarios to understand when to step up and when to step back.

Birds Uuable to Fly

When you find a bird on the ground and unable to fly, what to do depends on the age of the bird and the circumstances.

1. **Fledgling:** If he is fully feathered and hopping/fluttering without injury, leave him be. His parents are likely nearby.
2. **Hatchling:** If he has sparse down, closed eyes, and is unable to move well, look for a nearby nest and return him. If you cannot locate the nest or it's too high to reach, place the hatchling in a small container lined with soft fabric and hang it near where you found him, preferably in a tree or shrub. Leave the scene, and keep pets and predators away.

3. **Injured:** If a bird is on the ground and unable to move or fly, carefully place her in a ventilated box with soft lining. Contact your local wildlife rehabilitator or animal services for assistance.

4. **Stunned:** If you find a bird lying on the ground, stunned from having flown into a window, first check for injuries. If there aren't any, place her in a ventilated cardboard box and leave her in a safe, quiet spot outside. After 30–60 minutes, check again. If she still can't fly, contact a wildlife rehabber.

While it's best to avoid prolonged interaction with any wild animal, it's a myth that parents will reject their young if touched by a human.

Baby Mammals

When you come across a baby deer (or a baby rabbit) all alone, it's natural to want to help. Our compassionate instincts, however, might not always be what's best for the baby or her mother.

What a lot of people don't know is that it is perfectly normal for baby deer (and rabbits or hares) to be left alone without their mothers for several hours at a time. Leaving them in a thicket or tall grass, the mother will go off to forage for food knowing that her offspring are safe where she left them. The baby knows to remain still and hidden until his mother returns, which can take several hours—sometimes even up to twenty-four hours.

It may look as if they're abandoned, but they do not need assistance unless there are signs of present danger.

1. Observe her behavior from a distance. If she appears healthy, just leave her be. A healthy fawn will be alert and may stand up and walk around a little bit, but she will not be overly active or wandering around aimlessly. She may cry sporadically but not much. She knows to avoid attracting predators.

2. However, your intervention may be needed if the mother is clearly dead or if the baby is:
   - lethargic, weak, or disoriented;
   - cold, wet, or dirty with diarrhea or fly larvae;
   - crying or screaming out for prolonged periods of time;
   - visibly injured or visibly underweight;
   - following people and even attempting to nibble them;
   - lying prostrate—legs/head outstretched on the ground.

In those cases, you will want to contact the nearest permitted wildlife rescue / rehabilitator (keep their number in your phone contacts for such emergencies), and follow their suggestions. This goes for any baby animal you may find: observe, and get expert guidance, if need be.

If it's necessary to intervene, always approach slowly, wrap them lightly in a towel, and place them in a ventilated box until you can get them to a wildlife hospital. Call first to make sure someone will be there to receive you.

Adult Mammals

Generally speaking, if an adult wild animal lets you get close, something is definitely wrong, but whether it's a deer, an opossum, a raccoon, or a skunk, there are still ways to provide aid.

- Take photos or videos, if possible. These can be immensely helpful when trying to assess what is wrong, especially when you can't or shouldn't get close enough.
- Seek the guidance of a wildlife rescue organization. Even if you don't have a local wildlife rehabber nearby, find one online you can call. Whomever you reach, share the photos or videos with them so they can better understand the situation.
- If you are confident it is safe for you to capture the injured animal and bring him to a wildlife center, do so carefully, quietly, and with gloves. Have a towel-lined box ready, and minimize talking and noise.

Sometimes the best thing you can do is call animal services to euthanize the animal in order to relieve their suffering. It's not the outcome anyone wants, but it can often be the most humane solution.

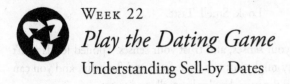

Play the Dating Game
Understanding Sell-by Dates

One of the leading causes of food waste is confusion over food expiration dates—confusion that benefits no one but food manufacturers.[23] Once they sell an item to a grocery store, it's out of their hands, and they can sell more when stores discard their products.

In fact, grocery stores toss out *huge* quantities of edible food for this reason, and since that food is packaged, tons of plastic and nonbiodegradable packaging are sent to dumps as a result, where they will languish for hundreds of years either on land or in the ocean, or break down into microplastics that human and nonhuman animals ingest.

While we have all come to believe that the "sell by" dates on labels are regulated and exist to protect us from foodborne illnesses, neither is true. Date labels on food are not standardized, and they have almost nothing to do with food safety; they have more to do with the date by which the company deems the food to be as "fresh" as possible. It's just a *recommendation* from the food manufacturer; it is not *mandated* by any federal food safety law.

What makes it even more confusing are the labeling inconsistencies from manufacturer to manufacturer; one product might say "best by," another might say "sell by," and yet another might say "best if used before." They all have different meanings, but the average consumer—unaware of the differences and understandably wary—interprets these "sell by" dates to mean that a product past that date is expired, spoiled, and unsafe to eat.

It's not—necessarily.

Because of this confusion and the unnecessary waste and expense it causes, nonprofit organizations as well as food industry trade groups have been trying to persuade food manufacturers and retailers to abolish the confusing labels altogether or to use clearer labeling language such as "best if used by" or "freshest if used by."

So, while work is being done to change things on the back end, when it comes to understanding what these labels mean on products in your own home, here is a simple guide:

Look. Smell. Taste.

In other words, use your senses, and trust your senses. Spoiled foods aren't necessarily *hazardous*; they might just not be as fresh and flavorful, and you can determine this yourself by the way they look, smell, and taste:

- if there's mold on your leftovers;
- if a several-month-old carton of coconut milk yogurt looks runny and tastes more sour than it should;
- if several-years-old spices have no fragrance at all.

Yes, this is a subjective test, but our senses have developed over thousands of years to warn us about the presence of potential harmful substances. For example, bitter tastes can indicate poisons, and a sour taste and unpleasant smell can indicate spoiled foods that should be avoided.

What *is* relatively new, however, is our ability to store foods and keep them fresh for future consumption, increasing food security and food safety, but we've got work to do in this area as well, because improperly storing food is another top cause of food waste, which is addressed in Week 50: Prolong Shelf Life.

WEEK 23

Build Muscle.

Don't Eat It.

Think about how many people you have heard of with high blood pressure, high cholesterol, diabetes, heart disease, or cancer. Perhaps you know some of them directly. Perhaps you experience any number of these conditions yourself. Perhaps you have been prescribed medications to treat them.

Now, think about how many people you know with kwashiorkor. How many hospitals have you been to with kwashiorkor wards? How many kwashiorkor specialists have you consulted? Probably none, and that's a good thing.

Kwashiorkor is the scientific term for protein deficiency, a severe acute malnutrition characterized by a lack of protein intake in the diet. Symptoms of kwashiorkor include swelling (edema) in the legs and feet, along with a distended abdomen, skin lesions, and a failure to grow and develop properly. It can lead to serious complications if left untreated, including impaired immune function, stunted growth, and even death. It typically occurs in young children, especially in poverty-stricken countries where people routinely have a limited supply of food.

Considering how obsessed we are with the consumption of *animal* protein, you'd think kwashiorkor would be rampant among people who eat only plants; i.e., vegans. But it isn't, because true *protein deficiency* is very rare in economically developed countries where food scarcity is not the problem.

In fact, diseases of deficiency are virtually a thing of the past. How many people do you know with scurvy (vitamin C deficiency), rickets (vitamin D deficiency), or beriberi (vitamin B1 deficiency)? These are pretty minor concerns in our current healthcare system. But how many millions of people in wealthy nations suffer from high blood pressure, high cholesterol, type-2 diabetes, heart disease, cancer, and gout? These are *major* health concerns—all of which are considered *diseases of excess* not *diseases of deficiency*, and all of which have been linked to the consumption of meat, dairy, and eggs—not plants.

The issue isn't that plants don't contain enough protein. The issue is that most people are consuming *too much* animal protein. According to the US Department of Agriculture, most Americans consume more animal protein than they need, and overconsumption of protein, particularly from animal sources, is associated with an increased risk of various health problems, including heart disease, cancer, and kidney damage. As a result, revised Dietary Guidelines for Americans have advised for the first time that men and teenage boys, in particular, should reduce their consumption of meat, chicken, and eggs—and increase their consumption of vegetables.[24]

It's not that protein isn't a necessary nutrient for building muscle. Of course it is, but we don't need to *consume* muscle in order to *build* muscle. We can do so by eating a variety of nutrient-, vitamin-, mineral-, protein-rich plant foods.

In short, there are 20 amino acids that make up the *building blocks* of protein—11 are nonessential (those that can be made by the body), and 9 are essential (those the body cannot produce on its own and so which must be obtained from the diet).

Essential amino acids are in all plant foods; some plant foods just have higher amounts of amino acids than others. And some plant foods contain *all* of the essential amino acids, namely quinoa, buckwheat, amaranth, and soybean-based foods such as tofu, tempeh, and edamame. But even if you never consume these particular foods, you can easily meet your protein and amino acid needs by eating a *variety* of whole plant foods throughout each day—fruits, vegetables, nuts, seeds, beans, lentils, and grains, all of which also provide the vitamins, minerals, fiber, folate, antioxidants, and phytochemicals that enable us to live and thrive.

How Much Protein Do We Need?

Current guidelines for protein consumption vary based on age, sex, physical activity level, and specific life stages. Here are the general recommendations from major health organizations, including the US Department of Agriculture (USDA) and the US Department of Health and Human Services (HHS), which set nutritional guidelines.[25]

General Population (Adults): Current guidelines recommend that adults consume 0.36 grams of protein per pound of body weight per day. This is approximately:

- If you weigh 150 pounds: 150 × 0.36 = 54 grams of protein per day.
- If you weigh 200 pounds: 200 × 0.36 = 72 grams of protein per day.

These guidelines are for the average sedentary adult. As noted below, protein needs may be higher for athletes, pregnant women, or individuals with specific health goals.

Older Adults: Many health experts suggest that adults aged 60 and over may benefit from higher protein intake to help maintain muscle mass and strength. Recommendations often range from 0.45 to 0.54 grams of protein per pound of body weight per day.

Athletes and Active Individuals: Competitive athletes or those with high levels of physical activity generally also need more protein to support muscle repair and growth: 0.54 to 0.91 grams per pound of body weight per day, depending on the intensity and type of exercise.

Pregnant and Lactating Women: Pregnant and breastfeeding women require more protein to support fetal development and milk production:

- 0.5 grams per pound of body weight per day during pregnancy.
- 0.59 grams per pound of body weight per day during lactation.

Children and Adolescents have varying needs depending on the age:

- Children aged 1 to 3 years: 13 grams per day
- Children aged 4 to 8 years: 19 grams per day
- Children aged 9 to 13 years: 34 grams per day
- Boys aged 14 to 18 years: 52 grams per day
- Girls aged 14 to 18 years: 46 grams per day

These recommendations are the same for vegans and non-vegans. The only difference is the sources of protein—not the amounts themselves. Let's take a look at the protein content in a range of plant-based sources—from whole foods to convenience foods to protein powders. (The Food Database of the United States Department of Agriculture provided all of these data.)

- Seitan (Wheat Gluten): 1 cup, 75 grams
- Peanut Butter: 1 cup, 65 grams
- Soybeans (cooked): 1 cup, 30 grams
- Tempeh (cooked): 1 cup, 30 grams
- Peanuts: ½ cup, 19 grams
- Lentils (cooked): 1 cup, 18 grams
- Beans (cooked): 1 cup, 15 grams
- Sunflower Seeds: ½ cup, 15 grams

- Almonds: ½ cup, 15 grams
- Pumpkin Seeds: ½ cup, 12 grams
- Tofu: ½ cup (extra-firm), 10 grams
- Oats (quick-cooking): 1 cup, 10 grams
- Green Peas (cooked): 1 cup, 9 grams
- Quinoa (cooked): 1 cup, 8 grams
- Mushrooms (cooked): 1 cup, 6 grams
- Brown Rice (cooked): 1 cup, 5.5 grams
- Chia Seeds: 3 tablespoons, 5 grams
- Sweet Corn (cooked): 1 cup, 4.8 grams
- Whole Wheat Bread: 1 slice, 4 grams
- Potato (baked with skin): 1 cup, 2.7 grams
- Broccoli (raw): 1 cup, 2.6 grams

Even a banana has a gram of protein. Finally, let's look at the impressive amount of protein in plant-based meats, which are enjoyed by vegans and non-vegans alike.

Plant-Based Meats

- Impossible Burger: 19 grams of protein per 4-ounce patty
- Beyond Burger: 20 grams of protein per 4-ounce patty
- Tofurky Sausage: 29 grams of protein per sausage (113 grams)
- Gardein Ultimate Beefless Burger: 20 grams of protein per 3.4-ounce patty
- Lightlife Smart Dogs: 7 grams of protein per hot dog (45 grams)
- Field Roast Sausages: 25 grams of protein per sausage (92 grams)

Protein Powders

While there are plenty of plant-based protein powders on the market, be sure to check ingredient labels for animal-derived ingredients like whey, casein, collagen, or egg whites. To ensure that it's fully plant-based, look for products labeled "vegan" or "plant-based." Here are several of my favorite brands whose products feature diverse flavors along with variations in protein content, ranging from 15 to 30 grams of protein per serving.

- Vega
- Complement
- Garden of Life

So, build muscle with healthful, nutrient-rich plants—just like the strongest and largest animals on the planet do—but also build muscle with *weights*.

Resist!

Scientific research consistently supports weight resistance training as one of the most effective ways to build muscle mass and strength—either with free weights, gym machines, resistance bands, or your own body weight.

Aside from building muscle, research shows that resistance training also increases longevity, alleviates feelings of anxiety and depression, enhances balance and flexibility, aids in weight control, lowers the chances of injury, and enhances cardiovascular health. This is why the Centers for Disease Control and Prevention recommend spending at least two days a week on muscle-strengthening activities, gradually increasing the resistance, repetitions, or sets over time to continue challenging your muscles and promoting strength gains.

Stop Acting Like a Baby (Cow)

If you didn't take a 30-Day Vegan Challenge as previously recommended in Week 14 or are just taking things slowly, now is at least a good time to wean yourself from cow's milk—assuming, of course, that you're not a baby calf. Whether you want to optimize your health, avoid animal cruelty, or prevent environmental degradation, switching to plant-based milks ticks all those boxes.

No animal continues to drink their species' milk into adulthood—not human animals, not nonhuman animals. In fact, the thought of consuming our own mother's milk or products made from it (like ice cream, yogurt, or cheese) is grossly unappealing to most people.

So is the idea of drinking milk from dogs, cats, or rats. Dog's milk? No way! Cat's milk? Heck no! Rat's milk? Now you're just talking nonsense. Cow's milk? Bring it on!

Clearly, part of our disgust comes from the fact that we intuitively recognize that rat's milk is for baby rats, cat's milk is for kittens, dog's milk is for puppies, and human milk is for human infants, but after centuries of conditioning, we have normalized the human consumption of milk from cows, goats, sheep, and other herd animals.

Pro-dairy marketing has convinced us that not only is it *normal* and *natural* to consume the milk of other animals, it's also healthy and humane. A closer examination of scientific research and ethical considerations, however, reveals an entirely different story. Let's look first at the animal welfare concerns.

Despite the pastoral scenes we all grew up with, there is simply no way to farm animals without compromising their well-being. This is especially true when it comes to dairy cows, whose short lives consist of a cycle of forced pregnancies, physical discomfort, and loss. A cow is impregnated starting at about fifteen months old. By age five, she will have undergone three or four pregnancies and been separated from all her calves. If her calves are male, "nonproductive" as they are in an industry that exploits the female reproductive system, they are killed immediately or within sixteen weeks and sold as veal. If her calves are female, they are subjected to the same fate as their mother.

Because the value of a cow's life is tied to her ability to produce offspring and thus produce milk, when the cost of feeding, medicating, and sheltering her exceeds the profit from her milk, she is sent to slaughter. Although cattle can live fifteen to twenty years, dairy cows are typically slaughtered at four to five years old. This happens regardless of whether the farm is small, organic, "humane," or family-owned. No matter how the milk is labeled—organic, whole, pasteurized, unpasteurized, homogenized, raw, lactose-free, low-fat, 2 percent, 1 percent, skim, fat-free, rBST-free, or natural—dairy cows are all eventually sent to slaughter.

There is no such thing as slaughter-free animal agriculture, even for those animals bred and raised for their milk or eggs.

From a health perspective, the consumption of dairy products has been implicated in both discomfort and diseases, including gastrointestinal distress and acne, as well as an increased risk of cancer, cardiovascular diseases, type-1 *and* type-2 diabetes, and osteoporosis.[26] What's more, because they're mammals like us, cows' milk naturally contains such hormones as estrogen and progesterone, as well as growth hormones such as insulin-like growth factor 1 (IGF-1), which have been linked to hormone-related cancers and early puberty in children.

As we discussed in Week 11: Skip the Middle Animal, although calcium is essential for strong bones, dairy products are not. The animal protein in dairy can increase the acidity of urine, which the body neutralizes by using calcium from bones, leading to higher calcium loss. It's better to obtain calcium from green leafy vegetables, which are rich in highly bioavailable calcium. Note that the calcium content in vegetables can vary significantly between their cooked and raw forms due to water loss during the cooking process. When vegetables are cooked, they lose a significant amount of water, which concentrates the nutrients like calcium into a smaller volume. This is why the milligrams of calcium appear higher in cooked versions despite using the same starting quantity of the vegetable. (The Food Database of the US Department of Agriculture provided all of the following data.)[27]

- **Collard Greens:** One cup cooked contains about 268 milligrams of calcium; one cup raw contains approximately 84 milligrams.
- **Kale:** One cup cooked contains around 177 milligrams of calcium; one cup raw contains about 53 milligrams.
- **Bok Choy:** One cup cooked contains approximately 158 milligrams of calcium; one cup raw contains about 74 milligrams.
- **Chard:** One cup cooked contains approximately 102 milligrams of calcium; one cup raw contains approximately 18 milligrams.

- **Broccoli:** One cup cooked contains approximately 62 milligrams of calcium; one cup raw contains about 43 milligrams.

Apart from leafy greens, there are a number of high-calcium plant foods, including:

- **Blackstrap molasses:** 191 milligrams of calcium per tablespoon;
- **Soybeans:** 175 milligrams of calcium in one cup;
- **Almonds:** 92 milligrams of calcium per quarter cup;
- **Figs:** 90 milligrams of calcium per five pieces;
- **Tempeh:** 92 milligrams of calcium in one half cup.
- All legumes have impressive amounts of calcium but some have higher amounts than others. Soybeans are the highest, containing about 175 milligrams per cup of cooked beans. Navy beans are next with about 126 milligrams per cup of cooked beans; and Great Northern are just behind with approximately 121 milligrams of calcium per cup of cooked beans.

And finally, just as cow's milk is fortified with calcium and other nutrients, so are some common commercial products and plant-based foods:

- Many breakfast cereals, such as Total, Special K Plus, and some oatmeal brands, are fortified with calcium. The calcium content can vary by brand and product, but the range is usually 600 to 1,000 milligrams of calcium per one cup.
- Plant-based milks vary, but they hover around 300 milligrams of calcium per cup, equivalent to cow's milk.
- One cup of calcium-fortified orange juice also offers about 300 milligrams of calcium.
- The calcium content in tofu can differ depending on the brand and the type of coagulant used to make it. Firm tofu made with calcium sulfate typically has a high calcium content (about 900 milligrams per cup). To determine the calcium content of tofu, simply check the label.

Relying on plant foods for calcium means you also amplify a myriad of health benefits because those same foods contain a plethora of essential vitamins, minerals, fiber, folate, antioxidants, and phytochemicals, and they are devoid of unnecessary and unhealthy saturated fats, dietary cholesterol, casein, and lactose. Win–win.

Speaking of upsides to choosing plant milks over animal milks, from an environmental perspective, cow's milk emits three times more greenhouse gases, needs around ten times more land, and requires twenty times more water than any plant milk, whether it's made from nuts (almonds, hazelnuts, peanuts, cashews), grains (oats, rice, quinoa), legumes (soybeans and peanuts), or seeds (coconut, hemp, sunflower).[28] Whatever you choose, you're giving a gift to your health, the animals, and the Earth.

Focus on the Method, Not the Milk

Obviously, cow's milk doesn't only take the form of a liquid. It's also:

- coagulated to make cheese;
- curdled to make buttermilk;
- churned to make butter;
- cultured to make yogurt;
- fermented to make sour cream.

All of these processes can be (and are) applied just as effectively to plant milks as well. There's nothing inherently unique about animal milks that makes them more suitable for these transformations.

I make this point because foods made from plant-based milks are often derided for being inferior at best and "fake" at worst, compared with those made from animal-derived milks. Part of the problem is that we're contrasting something that is familiar with something that is new, in which case the former will always win. If, instead, we regarded plant-based foods on their own terms, it would be an entirely different story; we would appreciate them for being *different from* rather than *subordinate to* animal products. But more than that, we would recognize that it's the *methods*—not simply the milk—that create the desired derivatives. For instance:

- coagulate plant milks, and you also get cheese (and tofu);
- curdle plant milks, and you also get buttermilk;
- churn plant fats, and you also get butter;
- culture plant milks, and you also get yogurt;
- ferment plant milks, and you also get sour cream.

Same processes. Different milks.

Of course, there are some differences in the *source* of these processes—different types of coagulants, different types of cultures, various means and methods.

- **Coagulation:** Coagulants are substances that cause milk proteins to clump together, essentially separating the curds (solid fats) from the whey (the remaining liquid), as Little Miss Muffet so famously did. They can be derived from various sources, including rennet (from the lining of calves' stomachs), microbes (through fermentation), acids (such as vinegar and citric acid), salts (such as epsom), and sulfates (from magnesium or calcium). Depending on the coagulant used, you get a different result.
- **Culturing and Fermenting:** Whether derived from microbes, yeasts, molds, lactic acids, or bacteria, different cultures are used to make different products, depending on the culture used and result desired. While some cultures are derived from animals, not all are, and vegetable-derived cultures are commonly used in the cheese industry (just as vegetable-derived rennet is also used even in cheeses made from animal milk).

Of course, other factors such as milk composition, aging processes, emulsifiers, and environmental conditions all contribute to the vast array of flavors and textures found in different cheeses, creams, and butters, and that's the case even when your base is milk derived from plants. These are not fake, faux, mock, imitations, analogs, or substitutes. They're *real* food based on *real* ingredients.

Finally, it's worth saying that the reason we drink the milk of some animals and not others is completely arbitrary. If high amounts of calcium, protein, and fat were our criteria, we would have domesticated *hyenas*, who have the highest concentration of these nutrients in their milk (they do, after all, eat bones). The animals we domesticated—whether for their meat, milk, or muscles —are mostly herd animals—cattle, goats, sheep, buffalo, camels, yaks, llamas, alpacas, reindeer, horses, and donkeys. That means they're easy to control, and they're easy to confine. In other words, we drink their milk and eat their meat not because of the nutritional quality of their flesh and fluids, but because of the behavioral characteristics of their species.

The agricultural revolution that began 11,000 years ago dramatically and permanently altered our relationship to and interaction with animals. But it's not too late to make better choices, more compassionate choices, once we know better. It's time to get ourselves off of the milk of other animals and enjoy the fats, ferments, and fluids of milks derived from plants.

Your Fridge Is Not a Compost Bin

Eat Leftovers

There are two kinds of people in this world—those who eat leftovers and those who aspire to but who leave them languishing in the refrigerator until they are no longer recognizable as eatable edibles.

Okay, there are probably more than two types of people in this world, but truly, when it comes to leftovers, I often find that people either love them or hate them. Why do people respond so differently? Experts who study the psychology of leftovers assert that a number of factors are at play—some related to food safety, some related to finances, some to sustainability, and some to cooking confidence.

Whatever it is that compels some people to embrace leftovers and others to shun them, we're clearly not "wired" one way or another. Even though humans have been fermenting, canning, pickling, and otherwise preserving foods for thousands of years, it wasn't until refrigeration came along in the 1920s and 1930s that it became possible to prolong the life of foods in their *fresh* state. Initially, only affluent families were able to afford refrigerators in their homes, so keeping leftovers was actually a sign of prestige.

Over time, as refrigerators became commonplace in people's kitchens, leftovers lost their luster. And while food safety is certainly on some people's minds when they question whether or not to eat leftovers, for others, it's simply a matter of not wanting to eat the same thing several days in a row. My husband is one of those people; I am not.

While David sees leftovers as representing a lack of variety and choice, I see them as the potential to be transformed into something new and even tastier than the original.

Regarding food safety, hopefully I've mitigated your concerns and boosted your confidence in this area (see Week 22: Play the Dating Game): trust your senses, use labels as a *suggestion* about freshness not as an indication of danger, check the temperature of your fridge, and keep food in airtight containers.

But when it comes to avoiding leftovers because you think they're boring or unappealing, the solution is to *reinvigorate* them. One way is simply to heat them up or add additional spices and salt. Another way is to transform them into something new and delicious.

- Transfer leftover soups to a saucepan, cover and heat over medium-low until the liquid reaches a gentle simmer. Add *additional* spices (cumin, chili powder, curry powder, pepper, paprika, etc.), or throw in some cooked noodles, rice, or quinoa. Sprinkle with fresh herbs. There is *nothing* fresh herbs can't revitalize.
- Heat up pizza for 10 minutes in a convection oven at 350°. (Reheated pizza is the best!)
- Turn stale bread into croutons, breadcrumbs, or French toast.
- Cube day-old bread to make Panzanella Salad (aka "bread salad") with tomatoes, oil, vinegar, and fresh herbs.
- "Scramble" cooked polenta in a sauté pan with chopped onions and peppers.
- Turn mashed potatoes into potato pancakes, sauté them in onions and garlic for a delicious "hash," or make homemade gnocchi.
- Make a sloppy sandwich out of leftover stir-fried vegetables. Add lettuce, avocado slices, and eggless mayonnaise.
- Make no-queso quesadillas from leftover hummus and salsa. Just spread hummus and salsa on one side of a flour tortilla, place it face up in a sauté pan and add another tortilla on top. Once it's golden brown on one side, flip it and cook until golden brown on the other.
- Revive boring brown rice in a pan with soy sauce, fresh ginger, and chopped veggies. Top with sliced scallions.

What seems at first glance a *boring repeat* becomes a *brand-new dish*. It just takes a little creativity and imagination—and a willingness to eat them. By turning lemons into lemonade—*literally*—we save money, we save resources, and we save animals who would otherwise be attracted to our garbage cans.

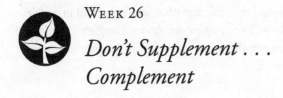

WEEK 26

Don't Supplement . . . Complement

In the pursuit of optimal health and well-being, the importance of vitamins and minerals cannot be overstated. However, in our quick-fix society, we have been conditioned to believe that we can offset an unhealthy lifestyle with a daily dose of supplements and that the beneficial properties of whole foods can be contained in a single tablet. There's a reason the global dietary supplements market is a multibillion-dollar industry.

Nature is a complex system, and no single nutrient works in isolation in our bodies. All the nutrients in plants—fiber, phytonutrients, vitamins, and minerals—work together as a cohesive package. So just isolating nutrients and taking them as a pill means you're missing out on the complexity of what makes plant foods so beneficial.

But that doesn't mean we can't take advantage of modern miracles.

As we've industrialized, we've shifted away from diseases of deficiency (scurvy, rickets, beriberi, kwashiorkor) to diseases of affluence (cancer, heart disease, and diabetes—particularly type-2), and isn't it remarkable that with a few lifestyle adjustments and access to essential nutrients, we have the potential to become the healthiest generation yet, free from nutritional deficiencies.

In other words, though the best place to get the majority of our vitamins, minerals, phytonutrients, folate, and antioxidants is from whole foods (and the sun), many health experts still advocate taking additional supplements—not as a *substitute* for good nutrition but as a *complement* to it. Supplements don't have to come in the form of a *multivitamin* per se; research shows that most of the vitamins in a multivitamin are unnecessary (such as vitamin C), potentially harmful (such as vitamins A and E), are needed only during specific situations (e.g., folic acid during pregnancy), or are needed to reverse a particular deficiency (e.g., iron when anemia is present). So the best advice would be to take supplements only for the single nutrients you need to boost. You can determine this by getting a blood and urine panel done by your health professional and make adjustments accordingly.

Here are some vitamins and minerals that often aren't plentiful in our daily diets and that we would do well to *complement*. And remember: vitamin and mineral deficiencies exist among the general population—vegetarians, vegans, pescetarians, *and* meat-eaters.

Vitamin B12 (Cobalamin)

Vitamin B12 is crucial for maintaining healthy nerve cells, aiding in the production of DNA, and supporting red blood cell formation. Such a small amount is required that it's measured in micrograms; most synthetic supplements will have much more than the recommended amount, but that's not a problem, because it's a water-soluble vitamin and excess amounts are typically excreted in urine. According to the US Department of Agriculture (USDA) and the US Department of Health and Human Services (HHS), the recommended daily intake of vitamin B12 depends on age and lifestyle factors:

- **Infants to 12 months:** 0.5 micrograms (mcg) per day
- **Children 1 to 13 years:** 1.8 mcg per day
- **Teens and Adults:** 2.4 mcg per day
- **Pregnant and Lactating Women:** Between 2.6 and 2.8 mcg per day

Vitamin D

Vitamin D is a fat-soluble vitamin that helps absorb calcium (which is plentiful in a diet filled with leafy greens, beans, nuts, and seeds) and is essential for various bodily functions, but what makes it unique is that our bodies can produce it when our skin is exposed to sunlight. However, due to challenges in obtaining sufficient vitamin D from sunlight and diet alone, many people take vitamin D supplements to meet their needs.

The recommended daily intake of vitamin D can vary by age, sex, and life stage, but in general, it's recommended that adults up to age seventy have a daily intake of around 600 IU (International Units) and those above seventy years old increase that to 800 IU per day.

DHA (Omega-3 Fatty Acids)

Omega-3 fats are essential for overall brain health, improving memory and focus, and cardiovascular health. While there are no official guidelines for the intake of long-chain omega-3s, nutrition experts typically advise consuming 250 to 500 mg of long-chain fatty acids (combination of EPA and DHA) per day.[29]

Many manufacturers will use fish fats, but remember that, in Week 11: Skip the Middle Animal, we talked about the fact that fish don't naturally produce omega-3 fatty acids; they obtain them through their diet of algae or algae-eating krill and shrimp. So skip the middle fish and go straight to the source: DHA obtained from algae. (Most standard blood panels don't include omega-3 testing, but you can easily order home test kits to check your levels.)

Vitamins Best to Get from Food

Vitamin A

Many plant foods contain hundreds of carotenoids (one of which is beta carotene, which our bodies convert to vitamin A.) So pile on the sweet potatoes, carrots, kale, mangoes, spinach, turnip greens, winter squash, and collard greens.

Vitamin E

The best plant-based sources of vitamin E are nuts (such as almonds, hazelnuts, and sunflower seeds), seeds (like pumpkin seeds), leafy green vegetables (such as spinach and kale), avocado, vegetable oils (like wheat germ oil, sunflower oil, and safflower oil), fortified cereals, whole grains, tomatoes, broccoli, kiwifruit, and mangoes.

Vitamin C

Some of the top sources of vitamin C are indeed citrus fruits (lemons, limes, oranges, nectarines, grapefruit) but also a slew of other fruits and vegetables, including broccoli, bell peppers, kale, cauliflower, strawberries, mustard greens, turnip greens, Brussels sprouts, papaya, chard, cabbage, spinach, kiwi, snow peas, cantaloupe, tomatoes, zucchini, raspberries, asparagus, celery, pineapples, lettuce, watermelon, fennel, peppermint, and parsley.

Iron

It is generally recommended to obtain iron from food sources rather than supplements whenever possible. Good dietary plant sources of iron include beans, lentils, tofu, fortified cereals, and dark, leafy greens. If you are diagnosed with anemia, consult with your healthcare provider about whether supplements are necessary, but keep in mind that iron deficiencies can be effectively corrected without consuming animal flesh. Iron is a mineral, after all.

Increase Absorption

Speaking of *complementing*, as with all required nutrients that come from our diet, it is not simply a matter of taking in the nutrients. It's also a matter of absorbing and utilizing them. Our body's ability to absorb and utilize a nutrient from a food is called bioavailability. Here are some ways to increase the bioavailability of essential nutrients.

Complement Calcium with Vitamin D

To maximize calcium absorption, increase your vitamin D intake through exposure to sunlight or by taking supplements, especially if you're deficient or lack sun exposure. Light-skinned people should expose their face and forearms to ten to fifteen minutes of sunlight daily, while dark-skinned individuals may need three times as much. Commercial foods are sometimes fortified with vitamin D, including plant-based milks, orange juice, and breakfast cereals.

Besides boosting calcium intake and absorption, it's crucial to minimize calcium loss. Diet plays a significant role here, particularly protein and sodium intake, which can lead to calcium excretion. Plant proteins have fewer sulfur amino acids than animal proteins, but high protein intake can contribute to calcium loss—see Week 24: Stop Acting Like a Baby (Cow). Engaging in weight-bearing exercises also helps maintain strong bones.

Complement Iron with Vitamin C

One of the best ways to boost iron absorption is by eating vitamin C–rich foods alongside iron-rich foods. There are many tasty ways to combine these nutrients:

- Make a bean or lentil salad with lemon juice, chopped greens, and bell peppers.
- Toss a kale salad with olive oil, salt, white beans, barley, and slices of oranges or tomatoes.
- Bake a potato and top it with sautéed onions and peppers.

Just as there are ways to increase iron *absorption*, there are also factors that can *decrease* it. Consuming calcium supplements, coffee, or tea *alongside* iron-rich foods can inhibit iron absorption. Therefore, it's best to avoid these combinations if you're aiming to maximize iron absorption.

See Week 5: Eat by Color for more on how to increase the bioavailability of phytonutrients.

And if you're struggling to get into the habit of taking supplements, keep them in a place where you'll see them and be reminded to take them, such as by your toothbrush or morning tea. Finally, in terms of optimal nutrient absorption as well as to not irritate your tummy, take them with food.

Conscious Companion Animal Care
Choose Sustainable Products

From the toys they play with and the beds they sleep in, to the food they consume and the waste they produce, every aspect of caring for our dogs, cats, rabbits, and other companion animals contributes to their ecological pawprint. Let's examine three key areas—food, waste management, and enrichment—to see where we can reduce their environmental impact.

Eco-Friendly Enrichment

Zero waste doesn't mean never buying anything ever again; it means buying durable items that last—with warranties when possible and applicable. When it comes to toys, beds, and scratchers for our animals, many store-bought toys are made from plastic, which is a problem from cradle (petroleum extraction) to grave (nonrecyclable). Consider toys made from natural, organic, recycled, or other sustainable materials such as cotton, hemp, Tencel, or bamboo from eco-friendly brands. Or make them yourself when it's simple to do so.

Cats

Anyone who has ever had the pleasure of living with cats knows that they tend to derive more joy from packing materials than from the toys found inside the packaging. Cardboard boxes, paper bags, aluminum foil balls, and newspaper provide the texture and crinkly sound cats love. Not only are they free and easily attainable, they can also be recycled or composted once they're worn out. The same goes for cardboard scratchers and lounges, repurposed toilet paper and paper towel rolls, dried catnip stuffed into socks or fabric scraps, and found bird feathers (tie them onto a string and stick for a homemade wand toy). If you're looking for store-bought items, reach out to friends, neighbors, and thrift stores first; most people have unused toys lying around.

Dogs

Look for toys made from natural or recycled materials when possible, such as balls made from natural rubber, old T-shirts tied in knots, and repurposed fire hoses that can be used as chew toys. Consider sweet potato chews to satisfy their instinct for chewing (healthy, sustainable, and cruelty-free), and look to thrift stores, friends, and neighborhood groups for reusable toys.

Rabbits, Guinea Pigs, and Hamsters

Rabbits enjoy toys that stimulate their natural behaviors, such as chewing and digging. Safe options include cardboard tubes filled with hay or wooden chew toys made from untreated wood. These toys not only keep rabbits entertained but also help to wear down their teeth, which continuously grow. For other small animals like guinea pigs and hamsters, prioritize enrichment activities that encourage exploration and exercise—such as tunnels made from natural materials like hay or cardboard, as well as wooden chew toys that promote dental health.

Sustainable Sustenance

Herbivorous animals like rabbits, guinea pigs, hamsters, and turtles have the lowest eco footprint, but given that canines are omnivores (not carnivores), most dogs thrive on a plant-based diet, and most pet supply stores will offer a number of options for food and treats to choose from. Cats, on the other hand, are obligate carnivores and require meat and the amino acids contained within. Even so, there are many ways to "greenify" your feline household, starting with *you* basing *your* diet on plants.

Cats

As we've discussed (see Week 2), meat production requires vast amounts of land, water, and resources, making it much less sustainable than plant-based options. And while we humans can thrive on plants, cats do not. So, for those of us with rescue cats and foster cats, what are some ways we can mitigate their impact? Let's look at some potential solutions—some of which exist now, some of which are coming in the near future.

1. **Plant-Based Cat Food:** Some companies offer plant-based cat foods that aim to provide essential nutrition without animal-derived ingredients. While there are many anecdotal stories of cats thriving on plant-based diets, and more and more research being conducted in this area, not everyone is persuaded that even with amino acid supplementation, a 100 percent plant-based diet is the best thing for cats. But there may be

a work-around. Some pet guardians add 10 percent plant-based foods to their cats' diets alongside 90 percent animal-based proteins. This 90/10 approach can help reduce the overall environmental impact while ensuring that cats receive essential nutrients from animal sources.

2. **Better than Worst:** As we discussed in Week 2, the animal meats with the highest footprints are primarily beef and lamb, with pork following, and chicken and fish next. With that in mind, consider basing your cats' diet on animal proteins that are the least environmentally taxing. Of those, opt for products that use sustainably sourced ingredients. Look for certifications like MSC (Marine Stewardship Council) for fish products, or humane-grade, organic certifications for other ingredients.

3. **Future Foods:** Emerging technologies in cultured meat / cellular agriculture could potentially provide a sustainable and animal-friendly alternative. This involves growing meat from animal cells without the need to raise and slaughter animals. Insect proteins are also being explored as a sustainable alternative to raising and killing mammals and birds. Insects require significantly fewer resources to raise compared to livestock and can provide a protein-rich diet for cats.

Food Packaging and Serving

Depending on the brands you use, it may not always be possible to choose the most eco-friendly packaging. Personally, given the higher incidence of urological issues in cats who eat dry kibble, I feed my cats only canned food, which works out well given the fact that aluminum (and glass) is 100 percent recyclable. Thick, multilayer plastic bags that dry food comes in are not. (See Week 7 for companies that take hard-to-recycle plastic.) Additionally, choose metal, glass, or ceramic bowls for your animals' food and water. These materials have a lower carbon footprint, are durable, and won't need frequent replacing.

Waste Management

Now that we know what's going *in*, let's figure out what to do about what comes *out*! Ideally, all of our waste would be properly composted, though it's not something most people want to deal with. Composting dog, cat, and rabbit waste is possible but requires careful handling due to potential pathogens like toxoplasma (from cats) and E. coli (from all three). If you go this route, use a dedicated compost bin for pet waste only, ensuring that it's away from edible plants and follows local regulations. But generally speaking, when it comes to discarding waste, some methods are more eco-friendly than others.

Dogs

Use biodegradable poop bags made from materials like cornstarch or plant-based plastics. These bags break down more quickly in landfills compared to traditional plastic bags. You can also use newspaper.

Cats

Traditional clay litters are not biodegradable, contribute significantly to landfill waste, and often contain sodium bentonite, mined at the expense of natural landscapes. An alternative is plant-based litter, made from materials like wheat, corn, reclaimed wood, or recycled newspaper pellets. They vary in absorbency, with some being flushable in small amounts, are biodegradable and often come in recyclable packaging, minimizing a further environmental footprint.

(Many eco-friendly litters claim to be flushable, but there are important considerations. Cat feces should not be flushed, due to the risk of toxoplasmosis. *Toxoplasma gondii*, a parasite found in cat feces, can harm marine life like sea otters and sea lions, and it persists in the environment for long periods. Indoor cats who do not hunt or eat raw meat are unlikely to carry toxoplasmosis, and it's something you can test your cat's feces for.)

For cat litter boxes, ceramic or steel options are easier to clean and retain fewer odors than plastic ones.

Rabbits, Guinea Pigs, and Hamsters

Consider using bedding materials that are biodegradable and safe for composting, such as recycled paper or straw. When cleaning cages, avoid disposable plastic liners and instead opt for washable bedding or liners made from natural fibers. When disposing of waste, separate organic materials like soiled bedding from other trash to facilitate composting.

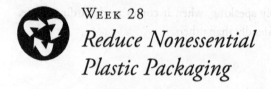

WEEK 28

Reduce Nonessential
Plastic Packaging

Plastic production has increased significantly over the past seventy years. In 1950, the global production was 2 million tons; today, it is a whopping 460 million tons—350 million of which becomes waste, 1 million of which ends up in the ocean, causing harm to wildlife and ecosystems.[30] To be sure, plastic provides several benefits: it's low-cost, durable, and crucial in medicine, construction, electronics, and food preservation. While it's impossible and impractical to eradicate plastic use altogether, there is a lot we can do to prevent it from polluting our water, air, and soil.

Large plastic items are also a problem because they eventually break down, and as they do, they don't simply disappear; they disintegrate into tiny particles called microplastics. While some microplastics are primary (such as microbeads used in personal care products), many are secondary—the result of the breakdown of plastic bottles, bags, and packaging materials as well as the shedding of tiny fibers from synthetic textiles like polyester and nylon, which make microplastics more prevalent than ever before. Their small size makes them easily ingestible by wildlife, which is a health hazard for them in general and a potential hazard for the people who ingest these animals.

Improper *disposal* is what turns plastic *use* into plastic *pollution*. (It's important to note that plastic *production* also generates air pollution and other environmental impacts, but this chapter is focusing on *discarded* plastic.) This is especially the case when it comes to our rivers, lakes, and oceans. The majority of the plastic waste going into waterways comes from the mismanagement of plastic waste on *land*, whether it's plastic bags, bottles, cutlery, or food packaging. That means 80 percent of land-based plastic waste is not being properly buried, recycled, or incinerated.[31] It also means that people don't take responsibility for their trash. They litter.

The next biggest contributor of plastic pollution in the ocean is maritime activities, primarily from the commercial fishing industry: fishing nets, ropes, lines, buoys, poles, dredges, traps, and other fishing and trawling gear.[32] For marine life, that means ingestion, injury, suffocation, and entanglement, all of which significantly increase an animal's likely mortality.

So what does this mean for each of us? What can we do individually to make a difference? Do we ban plastic bags? Banish plastic straws? Boycott plastic water bottles? Here are some solutions that would substantially reduce plastic waste in the ocean. Some may inspire you, some may surprise you, and while none of them is really very glamorous, they are what will make a difference.

1. Put pressure on governments to better regulate the commercial fishing industry by imposing penalties or fines on vessels that intentionally dump or abandon fishing and trawling gear.
2. Support policies that make *chemical* recycling more affordable. The current method employed by most countries is *mechanical* recycling, which means items can be recycled only once (maybe twice) before being degraded and eventually sent to a landfill. *Chemical* recycling means that items can be recycled endlessly (like glass), but at this time, it's a much more expensive process.
3. Advocate for government regulations that require plastic manufacturers to invest in chemical recycling and/or streamlining the plastics they make so that they are *actually* recyclable.
4. Support political candidates who prioritize waste-management policies—both domestically and as they relate to international trade.
5. Fund technology that intercepts waste before it gets to oceans in the first place.
6. Fund projects that help developing nations build infrastructure for proper disposal of waste.
7. Support policies that ban microbeads in personal care products.

I told you it wasn't sexy, but *how* waste is managed is in some ways more important than what the material is. That is to say, while plastic plays a useful role in our everyday lives, plastic *pollution* has no place at all.

However, there are some more *direct* things we can do individually that have the potential to have a great impact if we all step up collectively.

1. First and foremost, worry less about what type of bag you bring to the grocery store and focus more on what you put *in* that bag. In other words, if you are appalled with the plastic pollution caused by the fishing industry or worried about ingesting microplastics as they swim up the food chain, you can disengage from it by eliminating your consumption of aquatic animals, i.e., seafood.

2. If that's not going to happen, how about substantially *reducing* your consumption of seafood?

3. Just as we can quantify the environmental footprint of land animals (see Week 2: Eat Less Meat), we can do the same for the aquatic animals we farm and fish. Flounder, lobster, prawns, and shrimp have the highest footprint; bivalves (clams, oysters, cockles, mussels, scallops) and small wild fish (herrings and sardines) the lowest. However, by every measurement, plant foods have a smaller environmental footprint than any land or aquatic animals, whether they're fished or farmed.[33]

4. Don't litter! It really shouldn't have to be said, but I'm saying it. *Just don't litter.* Take responsibility for what is in your possession and dispose of it properly.

5. Use a microfiber filter or filter bag when washing your clothes to capture microfibers before they enter the wastewater system. (See recommendations in the back of the book.)

6. Participate in beach and shoreline cleanups to pick up trash before it makes its way into the ocean.

7. Explore alternatives to reduce your reliance on plastic for nonessential uses, such as plastic bottles, plastic plates, plastic cutlery, coffee cups with plastic lids, and prepackaged food and drinks.

   a. Invest in reusables: a stainless steel portable coffee cup, tea thermos, and water bottle will take care of all your beverage needs!

   b. Buy from bulk bins. You might think that there isn't a grocery store near you that has bulk bins for such things as beans, lentils, grains, and nuts, but do some sleuthing. You might be surprised by what you can find near you.

   c. Cook from scratch, at least some of the time. Visit Week 38: Cook from Scratch for recipes for some homemade staples, including plant-based milks.

   d. Switch to shampoo and conditioner bars.

   e. Support sustainable "zero-waste" refill companies like Plaine Products, from whom you can buy a variety of personal care items (shampoo, conditioner, body wash, hand wash), all which come in refillable aluminum bottles. After use, you simply return the empty containers using the prepaid label they provide, and Plaine Products washes, refills, and redistributes them.

   f. Opt for reusable bags for produce and for groceries to reduce the need for single-use plastic bags. While new cotton bags have their own environmental footprint, reusing what you have every time you shop will eventually offset the impact.

Living compassionately means embracing imperfection; it also means keeping things in perspective so that you don't give up entirely. Sometimes there are gray areas, and *better than bad* is *better than nothing*. Better is better. To summarize the most effective to least effective actions you can take:

Most effective: *stop eating seafood*
Least effective: *stop worrying about plastic straws*

Plastic straws account for maybe .02 percent of ocean plastics—literally a drop in the ocean compared to everything else.[34] Especially if you live in a wealthy country with a good waste-management system, the chances that your plastic straw will wind up in the ocean are very small.

Don't do nothing because you can't do everything, but focus on the big fish rather than the little fish. Oh, and as Nemo would surely support, just don't eat fish.

WEEK 29

Learn When to Choose Organic

The term "organic" often evokes idyllic images of pristine farms and a harmonious coexistence with nature. This romanticized perception suggests wholesome agricultural practices that use no pesticides, herbicides, or insecticides; have little to no negative environmental impact; and result in produce with higher nutrient density.

The reality is more complex.

The truth is: both organic and nonorganic systems have advantages and disadvantages depending on what you are measuring, and we can make informed decisions based on what the data show. Before we take a look at these findings, let's first clearly define the difference between organic and conventional agriculture.

- *Organic* agriculture involves cultivating crops (or breeding and keeping animals) without synthetic fertilizers, synthetic pesticides/herbicides, or genetically modified organisms. Organic agriculture does use chemicals, but they must be naturally derived and not synthetically manufactured.
- *Conventional*—also called *industrial*—farming involves using synthetically derived inputs (fertilizers, pesticides, herbicides, fungicides, insecticides) to enhance productivity, control invasive insects and diseases, and improve soil fertility.

Various large studies suggest that conventional agriculture outperforms organic methods when it comes to reduced land use, greenhouse-gas emissions, and water pollution for certain crops, but these studies also defy assertions that conventionally grown produce is less nutritious. When it comes to biodiversity, soil health, energy use, and pesticide concentration, organic has the upper hand—also depending on the crop.

There is no one-size-fits-all solution. Depending on the metrics we are looking at and the things we are solving for, we can find middle ground, make more-informed decisions, and stress less when it comes to our day-to-day purchases.

Land Use and Biodiversity: Organic farming requires more land compared to conventional farming primarily because natural inputs are less efficient than their concentrated synthetic counterparts. More land use increases deforestation and limits the scalability required to meet global food demand. On the other hand, conventional farming's synthetic pesticide use reduces biodiversity and insect populations.

Greenhouse-Gas Emissions: Overall, the greenhouse-gas emissions from organic and conventional farming systems seem to offset each other, but when all metrics are taken into account across all food crops and when you're faced with a choice, it might be a good idea to choose organically grown beans, lentils, and fruits, but conventionally grown grains and vegetables.

Energy Use: Organic farming typically requires less energy compared to intensive conventional farming because it avoids the use of synthetic chemicals. However, energy consumption in organic vegetable crops can be higher due to the use of propane-fueled flame weeding.[35]

Nutrient Density: Studies in epidemiology indicate that individuals who consume organic food tend to follow a healthier diet that includes more plant-based foods, fewer animal products, less soda, and less highly processed food compared to those who consume conventionally raised produce. However, decades of research has found that there is insufficient evidence to support the claim that organically grown foods are more nutritious; from a nutrients-per-dollar perspective, there's no definitive evidence that organic produce has a higher concentration of vitamins and minerals than conventionally grown produce.

Human Safety: While organic foods don't have more nutrients per dollar, one aspect of human health where organic has the advantage is in the health and safety of farm workers. Peer-reviewed studies have documented the serious health risks that farm workers who live near or work in conventionally grown crops face due to exposure to pesticides and herbicides, including increased incidences of various cancers, Type-2 diabetes, neurodegenerative diseases, birth defects, reproductive disorders, and other chronic health conditions. Studies linking the same diseases with regular consumption of pesticides are inconclusive, but experts argue that a precautionary approach would be prudent.

In the end there are trade-offs, and the idea is to make informed decisions without feeling guilty or stressed, but it's worth saying that the organic–conventional debate can be a distraction from what we know to be true:

- that in all the ways we can measure impact on our health, on the animals, and on the Earth, the negative effects of raising and eating any animal are far greater than those of growing and eating any plant—conventional or organic, land or aquatic.
- that any type of vegetable, fruit, grain, lentil, bean, mushroom, nut, or seed—however it's grown and however it's labeled—is better than none at all.

In other words: eat more plants.

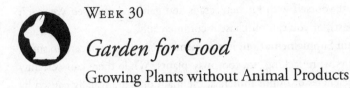

WEEK 30

Garden for Good

Growing Plants without Animal Products

Plants, like people, require essential nutrients—not animal products. (See Week 11: Skip the Middle Animal.) Just as we're told that we need to consume meat, dairy, and eggs when what we really need is protein, calcium, and omega-3 fatty acids (for example), so, too, are we told that our gardens need animal products such as bone meal, blood meal, feather meal, fish emulsion, and manure when what they really need is nitrogen, phosphorus, and potassium (and other vitamins and minerals).

Just as our health depends on a balanced diet and the nutrients we consume, plants rely on nutrient-rich soil as their primary source of sustenance to provide the foundational nourishment that allows plants to grow, develop strong roots, produce lush foliage, and bear abundant fruits or flowers.

For both plants and animals, supplements are valuable tools for addressing specific deficiencies or providing an extra nutrient boost (see Week 26: Don't Supplement . . . Complement), but they are not meant to *replace* the inherent richness of a healthy foundation.

For gardens, that foundation is the soil.

Whatever you're growing and however large your plot is—even if you only container-garden—there are several ways to go about ensuring nutrient-rich soil:

1. **Mulching:** Applying mulch to your garden beds helps retain soil moisture, regulate temperature, and reduce weed growth. Organic mulches also break down over time, which adds nutrient-rich matter to the soil.
2. **Plant Rotation:** Especially when growing vegetables, be sure to alternate the types of plants you grow in specific areas. This can help prevent nutrient depletion and minimize infestations and diseases.
3. **Composting:** Often referred to as "black gold" by gardeners, compost is a key component of a healthy garden and plays a vital role in promoting the growth of healthy plants, whether they're edibles or ornamentals. (It can also play the role of mulch, enriching your plants while also retaining water and regulating the temperature of the soil.) You can make

compost yourself with kitchen scraps and garden waste (see Week 47: Compost), or you can purchase it commercially.

4. **Nutrient Supplementation:** Just as *we* may need a boost of certain single nutrients we're lacking, so, too, may plants. While there can certainly be deficiencies of minor minerals, the main ones are usually caused by insufficient nitrogen, phosphorus, or potassium, collectively known as NPK. When you look at a box or bag of fertilizer, you'll find three numbers all in a row, which represent the NPK ratio. For example, a 24-6-6 fertilizer contains 24 percent nitrogen (N), 6 percent phosphorus (P), and 6 percent potassium (K) by weight. And while many commercial fertilizers will use animal products as the source of these nutrients, you don't have to.

- **Nitrogen (N)**, responsible for promoting leaf growth, is abundant in cottonseed meal, alfalfa meal, flaxseed meal, and soy meal.
- **Phosphorus (P)** supports root growth and flowering in plants. Phosphorus-rich fertilizers include rock phosphate or biochar, a type of charcoal created from plant matter.
- **Potassium (K)** is essential for enhancing a plant's disease resistance, and plant-based sources include kelp meal, seaweed, and wood ashes.

Most garden nurseries will sell these products, as well as animal-free blends like one called Vegan Mix 3-2-2 by a brand called Down to Earth. This balanced blend of essential nutrients nourishes plants without animal-based additives.

You can have your soil tested by a professional or by using a home test kit, but sometimes you can detect nutrient deficiencies just by *looking* at your plants, flowers, trees, and shrubs.

1. **Very Few Flowers:** If your plants have sparse blooms, especially during spring when they should be blossoming, it could indicate a lack of phosphorus.
2. **Yellowing Leaves:** Often a sign of a nitrogen deficiency, a nitrogen-rich compost could solve the problem, or a good dose of one of the meals above.
3. **Slow or Stunted Growth:** This may result from a lack of potassium.
4. **Browning Leaf Edges:** Calcium deficiency is indicated by brown edges. Lime or gypsum can correct this.
5. **Curling Leaves:** Boron-containing supplements can rectify this issue.

6. **Pale or Mottled Leaves:** Iron deficiency leads to chlorosis, presenting as pale or mottled leaves. Use chelated iron supplements to treat affected plants.
7. **Wilting:** Potassium deficiencies might lead to wilting, although water or root health issues can also cause it.

Plant health also means keeping certain critters from taking over and ravaging your crops and flowerbeds.

- **Snails:** Combat these garden intruders by hand-picking them or using copper barriers to deter them. When snails come into contact with copper surfaces or substances containing copper, they experience irritation and a burning sensation, prompting them to retreat or avoid the area.
- **Neem Spray:** Neem-based sprays serve as natural pesticides and effectively repel a wide range of unbeneficial garden invaders such as aphids, thrips, and whiteflies.

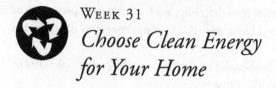

WEEK 31

Choose Clean Energy for Your Home

Over the centuries, our energy needs have largely been met by nonrenewable fossil fuels—petroleum, natural gas, and coal. While these resources have powered our economies and societies, they have come at a significant cost to our environment, health, and other animals. The burning of fossil fuels releases harmful pollutants into the air, along with greenhouse gases such as carbon dioxide, carbon monoxide, and methane. The consequences are well known and commonly felt: air pollution, smog, and respiratory illnesses, not to mention climate change and its related impacts.

To mitigate global warming and secure a sustainable future, the science is clear: we must eliminate our reliance on fossil fuels and instead get our energy needs met by renewables and other clean energy sources. Solar, wind, hydroelectric, and geothermal power, as well as nuclear power, produce minimal greenhouse-gas emissions and have fewer negative impacts on the environment and human health. Moreover, advancements in technology have made the use and storage of these renewable energy sources far safer, more affordable, and more accessible than ever before. (Research has shown that even despite the tragic events of Chernobyl in 1986 and Fukushima in 2011, nuclear power is substantially safer than burning fossil fuels or biomass).[36]

Some changes are hard to implement right away, some aren't in our budget right now, some are easy switcheroos. Here are large, small, and ongoing things we can do to conserve energy in our own homes, but one good place to start would be to conduct a professional energy audit of your home to identify areas for improvement. This is going to give you the most customized plan.

Biggest Impact

Heating and cooling are the primary energy consumers in our homes. Making any or all of these changes will have the greatest impact in terms of energy savings and cost savings. You may not be able to do these right away, but keep them in mind for future projects.

1. **Solar Panels:** Install photovoltaic solar panels on your roof to harness sunlight and convert it into electricity.
2. **Heat Pumps:** Replace traditional heating systems with heat pumps, which extract heat from the air, ground, or water to heat your home.
3. **Proper Insulation:** Make sure your home is well-insulated to maintain comfortable temperatures year-round without relying on artificial heating and cooling systems.

Every Bit Helps

Consider these upgrades as you continue to maintain your home or when you renovate.

4. **Double-Pane Windows:** Install double-pane or triple-pane windows to improve energy efficiency and reduce heat escaping through windows.
5. **Induction Cooktop:** Switch to an induction cooktop, which uses electromagnetic energy to heat cookware directly, wasting less energy and offering a more efficient and precise cooking method.
6. **Energy-Efficient Appliances:** When purchasing new appliances, look for energy-efficient models that have high Energy Star ratings. You can find these for such items as washers, dryers, dishwashers, refrigerators, freezers, and more.
7. **Energy-Efficient Landscaping:** Plant deciduous trees on the south- and west-facing sides of your house to provide natural shade in the summer. When their leaves drop in the winter, sunlight will provide natural warmth.
8. **Energy-Efficient Outdoor Lights:** For effectively lighting walkways and paths, solar lights have come a long way.

Small but Mighty Adjustments

9. **Window Treatments:** Use curtains, blinds, or shades to prevent heat loss in the winter and to keep indoor temperatures cooler in the summer.
10. **Air Leaks:** Seal gaps and cracks around doors, windows, and other openings with caulking or weather stripping to prevent leakage.
11. **LED Lighting:** Make the switch to LED light bulbs—they use less energy and last longer than traditional incandescent bulbs.

12. **Microwaves:** When possible, use your microwave. Not only are they perfectly safe from a health perspective, they are head and shoulders above conventional ovens in terms of energy efficiency, because they cook food faster and heat only the food (not the surrounding air).
13. **Get Smart:** Use smart home technologies to better control and regulate thermostats, lights, furnaces, and cooling systems.

Stay on track by continuously measuring your energy savings. Many energy companies now enable customers to track their day-to-day (sometimes hour-to-hour) energy use and consumption in order to make helpful tweaks.

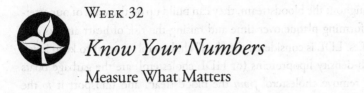

WEEK 32

Know Your Numbers

Measure What Matters

Just as we need to monitor our energy usage to be able to make beneficial alterations, so do we need to monitor our biomarkers to be able to do the same. Biomarkers—short for "biological markers"—are measurable indicators of various biological states, conditions, or processes within the body. Monitoring biomarkers provides valuable information about the body's physiological state and can be helpful in diagnosing diseases, monitoring disease progression, and predicting health outcomes.

While individual responses may vary, it is not uncommon to see tangible, measurable differences in certain biomarkers by eliminating meat, dairy, and eggs for just 30 days, physiological and biochemical changes that can be specifically tracked and measured. This is one of the reasons I recommend taking a 30-Day Vegan Challenge (see Week 14).

While you can use at-home monitoring devices for some biomarkers—such as for blood pressure and blood sugar—to get the most comprehensive picture, you will want to ask for a full blood and urine panel from your doctor or other health professional. Common laboratory tests span a wide spectrum, so I'm not including *all* of them here, but this is a good starting point.

Cholesterol

Naturally produced in the liver of animals, cholesterol is a fat-like substance that is essential for various physiological functions. Our livers make all the cholesterol we need, so it's not necessary to *consume* dietary cholesterol, which exists only in meat, fish, dairy, and eggs. *There is no dietary cholesterol in plant foods.* Plants, after all, don't have livers.

The cholesterol made by our bodies travels through the bloodstream via *lipoproteins.* Think of them as little boats delivering supplies and removing trash.

- Low-density lipoproteins (or LDL cholesterol) are the supply boats that deliver cholesterol *to* the cells, but if there are too many of them circulating throughout the bloodstream, they can build up on the walls of our arteries, forming plaque over time and raising the risk of heart attacks and strokes. LDL is considered the "bad" cholesterol we want to keep low.

- High-density lipoproteins (or HDL cholesterol) are the garbage boats that remove cholesterol *from* the bloodstream and transport it *to* the liver, which breaks cholesterol down and gets rid of it. HDL is considered the "good" cholesterol we want to keep high.

To determine cardiovascular disease risk, doctors look at *LDL, HDL,* and *total cholesterol.*

Total Cholesterol: Given the high average cholesterol level in the United States (around 200–220), recommendations suggesting lowering levels to "below 200" are still problematic.

- Decades of research, including landmark studies like the Framingham Heart Study and the China Study, emphasize that the optimal total cholesterol level should be below 150.
- The ideal level of LDL ("Bad") cholesterol is between 30 and 70 mg/dL.[37]
- The ideal level of HDL ("Good") cholesterol is between 40 and 60 mg/dL.

Triglycerides

Triglycerides are like cholesterol; they're fats made in the liver that circulate throughout the bloodstream. Though they're essential for many physiological functions, high levels are a risk factor for heart disease. The more triglycerides in the blood, the greater the likelihood of atherosclerosis (the building up of plaque in the arteries).

Levels of 200 to 500 mg/dL are considered dangerously high, raising the likelihood of a heart attack or stroke. The consensus in the medical community is to keep triglycerides between 50 and 150 mg/dL.

Homocysteine

Homocysteine is an amino acid broken down by vitamins B12, B6, and folate. When homocysteine is high, it may indicate a deficiency of these vitamins. Without getting those levels in check, there is an increased risk of cardiovascular disease, dementia, and stroke.

The optimal number is less than 10 micromoles per liter (µmol/L), up to 15.[38]

Blood Pressure

Blood pressure is a measure of how hard blood pushes against artery walls; think of it like water running through a hose. Blood pressure readings are made up of two values:

- *Systolic blood pressure* is the pressure on the heart when it *beats* and pumps blood *into* the blood vessels (the arteries, capillaries, and veins). *Systolic* comes from the Greek word meaning "contraction."
- *Diastolic blood pressure* is pressure on the arteries when the heart muscle relaxes between beats. *Diastolic* comes from the Greek word meaning "dilation."

When your blood pressure is measured, the top number indicates the systolic pressure, while the bottom number indicates the diastolic pressure, so if you have a blood pressure of 140/90 mmHg (millimeters of mercury), that means you have a systolic blood pressure of 140 mmHg, and a diastolic blood pressure of 90 mmHg.

While a blood pressure reading of 175 over 110 may be deemed "normal," research suggests a significant rise in the risk of stroke or heart disease with higher pressures. To minimize this risk, the recommended blood pressure level is ideally 110 over 70.[39]

Other biomarkers you can measure are blood glucose, body mass index, waist circumference, and liver and kidney function. Consult your health practitioner to get a full assessment.

Blood Glucose

Glucose, or blood sugar, is a key biomarker that indicates how well your body is managing sugar levels. High glucose levels can signal prediabetes (100–125 mg/dL) or diabetes (126 mg/dL or higher). Monitoring glucose is crucial for preventing diseases like type-2 diabetes, which is often related to lifestyle factors. A healthy fasting blood glucose range is typically 70–99 mg/dL. Regular monitoring and a whole-food, plant-based diet can help maintain healthy levels and reduce the risk of diabetes. Aim to keep fasting glucose below 100 mg/dL.

Regular blood tests are crucial for preventing disease because you can't improve what you don't measure. They help track key health markers, allowing for early intervention.

WEEK 33

Buy Cruelty-Free
Personal Care Products

It's amazing to still be talking about animal testing in the twenty-first century, but despite advancements in science and technology, millions of animals endure unimaginable suffering in laboratories all around the world.

While ensuring the safety of cosmetics and household products is crucial, testing on animals is archaic, unnecessary, and scientifically outdated. Animals from mice, rats, and rabbits to cats, dogs, and chimpanzees are subjected to a range of painful and distressing procedures, from skin irritation tests and eye irritancy tests to lethal-dose toxicity tests, whereby animals are force-fed or injected with chemicals, drugs, or other harmful substances until a dose is reached that kills 50 percent of the test subjects.

There are many more-sophisticated ways to test whether a substance is lethal to a human being—tests that are more reliable and more humane.

The use of animals in cosmetic testing traces back to 1938, when the Food, Drug, and Cosmetic Act was enacted in the United States. Since then, enormous progress has been made in alternative testing methods and animal welfare laws. A wide range of advanced technologies is now available, including computer modeling, predictive toxicology, in vitro human tissue, and organ-on-chip technology, all of which provide accurate and cruelty-free ways of assessing product safety without torturing animals.

At the time of publication, forty-five countries have either limited or banned animal testing for cosmetics, and as the public has become increasingly aware of the ethical issues and inefficacy of animal testing, the momentum for change continues to grow.[40] Here are some ways to support this progress:

- Look for products with the Leaping Bunny logo or the PETA Global Beauty Without Bunnies logo, certifications that guarantee a product has not been tested on animals at any stage of production.
- Apart from checking for the Leaping Bunny logo on the products themselves, you can visit the Leaping Bunny website (leapingbunny.org), which

contains a list of brands that reaffirm their commitment to cruelty-free practices every year.

- Patronize brands that use only synthetic or plant-based ingredients instead of animal-derived substances.
- Support legislation that bans cosmetic testing on animals and promotes the adoption of alternative testing methods.
- Share information about the cruelty of animal testing and the availability of cruelty-free alternatives with friends, family, and social media followers.
- Contribute to organizations that work to end animal testing and develop safe alternatives in the industry.

It's worth mentioning that being certified "cruelty-free" doesn't automatically mean a product is vegan, i.e., made without animal products. Even though a Leaping Bunny logo indicates no animal testing, a non-vegan product may still contain ingredients derived from animal farming or slaughter.

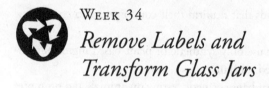

Remove Labels and Transform Glass Jars

When weighing the environmental footprint between glass and plastic, glass is the clear winner. Glass doesn't release harmful chemicals during its lifecycle; it's a durable material with a long lifespan, and it is truly renewable in that it can be recycled indefinitely without any loss in quality. (As we discussed in Week 28: Reduce Nonessential Plastic Packaging, if plastic were *chemically* recycled rather than *mechanically* recycled, it would indeed be able to be recycled endlessly.)

And yet, despite glass being 100 percent recyclable, an alarming percentage of glass set aside for recycling actually winds up in dumps. Of the 10 million metric tons of glass Americans throw away every year, only around one-third of it gets recycled.[41] Even if *you* are diligently following the rules and placing clean glass bottles and jars in their properly designated bin, most of them never see a second life.

Because of complex collection and sorting challenges, insufficient infrastructure, high transportation costs, fluctuating market dynamics, and the commingling of organic and nonorganic materials that leads to breakage and contamination, the recyclables we entrust to our cities' waste-management services are treated as so much garbage.

In other words, even though glass is legitimately and technically recyclable, we shouldn't rely on it as a solution. We must *reduce* and *reuse*.

One of the ways we can do this is by making things from scratch when we are able; this is not an option for every item we eat or drink—I don't make my own wine or spirits, for example!—but when it's easy enough to do so, we might consider relying more on some homemade staples. (See Week 38: Cook from Scratch.)

Another way to reduce glass packaging is by shopping at local stores that have refill stations. While more and more "zero-waste" stores are opening in cities all around the world, many natural food stores and regular supermarkets have bulk bins for such items as dried beans, lentils, nuts, seeds, and grains. For instance:

- Instead of buying new jars of peanut butter, bring an empty glass jar to the bulk section and refill it with peanut butter they make on-site.
- If that is not available, buy peanuts in bulk and make peanut butter from scratch, an easy process that requires only a food processor or blender.

So, first, *reduce*.

Next, *reuse*. For the glass jars and bottles we *do* buy, instead of treating them as a single-use vessel destined for the recycling bin, clean them, scrub off their labels, and *reuse* them.

One of the turning points for me in my zero-waste journey was when I stopped looking at a glass jar as a thing to be discarded and started seeing it as a thing to be used forever (or until it breaks). The idea that items should have *longevity* was a monumental perspective shift for me. I realized how ridiculous it is that we destroy perfectly functional glass bottles and jars in order to melt them down to make more perfectly functional glass bottles and jars—assuming they actually get recycled in the first place.

While governments, product designers, product manufacturers, and retailers must share responsibility, there are many things individuals *can* and *must* do in their own lives. I can't single-handedly solve the mammoth problem of overflowing landfills, limited recycling infrastructure, and unsustainable waste generation, but I continually remind myself daily of my go-to definition of waste:

Any item for which its owner has stopped taking responsibility.

Just as I'm responsible for a banana peel once I eat the banana, so, too, am I responsible for an empty glass jar or bottle once I consume its contents.

How to Remove Labels

Some labels are easy to remove; some are more difficult, but with my tips below and a little elbow grease, you should be able to succeed 100 percent of the time.

1. Soak your glass jar or bottle in warm soapy water for an hour or longer, at which time you may be able to simply scrape off what remains of the label glue with your fingernails, steel wool, or the flat side of a butter knife.
2. If the glue is stubborn, mix 1 part vegetable oil with 1 part baking soda, and smear it on the gluey bits. Let it sit for at least an hour. Then (without rinsing off the mixture), use steel wool or the abrasive side of a

kitchen sponge, and rub. A little scrubbing, a little soap and water, and a little more scrubbing has left me with beautiful glass bottles and jars.

Removing the label isn't *necessary*, but I prefer the clean look of label-free jars and bottles. Without marketing labels cluttering the containers, a pantry filled with label-free glass jars is just prettier—and even more practical. The clear, unadorned glass allows for a clear display of the contents within.

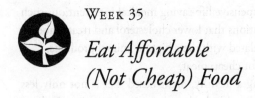

WEEK 35

Eat Affordable
(Not Cheap) Food

The myth that eating a healthy, plant-based diet is more expensive than eating an animal-based one is just that: a myth.

It's only because of large-scale industrialized animal farming and government subsidies and buy-backs that most people can afford to eat *every day* what are, in fact, *very expensive* things to produce. The problem isn't that healthy, whole, plant foods are too expensive; the problem is that unhealthy animal products are priced artificially *low*. People would eat substantially fewer animal products if they had to pay their true cost.

Meat, dairy, and eggs have *always* been products of privilege and symbols of affluence, affordable only by the rich and denied to the poor. This has been true historically, and it is true today, especially as countries become more modernized and industrialized.

Health-wise, that's turned out to be a good thing. In less affluent populations where animal flesh is served infrequently and in small quantities, the occurrence of heart disease, cancer, and diabetes—what experts refer to as "diseases of *affluence*"— is significantly lower.[42]

As wealth increases, so does the consumption of animal products, and so does the prevalence of the associated diseases, including Alzheimer's disease, atherosclerosis, asthma, cancer, chronic liver disease or cirrhosis, diabetes, gout, heart disease, high blood pressure, chronic renal failure, osteoporosis, stroke, depression, diverticulitis, and gallstones.

That's not to say that people of lower socioeconomic status don't get diseases of affluence; of course they do. Diseases of affluence afflict those with and without affluence. They're diseases without prejudice or concern for class, economic status, or race. Because of the mechanized food system peddling cheap food, *everyone*—wherever they are on the socioeconomic ladder—is eating the rich, fatty animal products that were once reserved for only the wealthy.

But because they often lack adequate healthcare coverage, people of lower socioeconomic status do tend to bear a heavier financial burden as they are forced to pay out of pocket for expensive life-saving medical interventions such as bypass surgeries, stents, medications that lower cholesterol and treat diabetes, or dialysis—all of which are correlated with diets high in animal products.

All in all, we pay high costs for cheap meat.

The good news is that eating a healthy, plant-based diet is not only less expensive in terms of healthcare costs, it's also less expensive day to day. Findings from numerous epidemiological studies, clinical trials, and meta-analyses consistently conclude that vegans tend to have lower blood pressure, lower cholesterol levels, and a lower risk of developing hypertension, type-2 diabetes, and certain cancers. And peer-reviewed studies have found that a plant-based diet is as effective as statin drugs in lowering LDL cholesterol levels—without the side effects.

When we look at the actual dollars-and-cents cost comparison between animal products and plant foods—even with government subsidies keeping animal products artificially cheap—whole plant foods are still less expensive than animal products. It's true that *convenience* foods are more expensive than whole foods, but that's the case whether the products are vegan or not, because you're paying for the *convenience* of a premade meal.

Luckily, our choices are not limited to "cheap animal-based hot dogs" versus "expensive veggie hot dogs." Our choices are also not limited to only *whole plant foods* versus only *highly processed convenience foods*. These are false dichotomies. Most of us eat a combination of whole foods, prepared foods, convenience foods, and restaurant foods. And it's up to each one of us which ones we favor over others day by day, depending on our preferences and our budget.

Here are some ways to make the most *affordable* choices—and the most *healthy* ones.

1. **Make Whole Foods the *Foundation* of Your Diet.** They don't have to comprise 100 percent of everything you eat, but the more you choose whole foods over more-processed, convenience foods, the more money you will save, and the more nutrient-dense your meals will be.
2. **Choose Nutrient-Dense Foods.** To further that point, hyper-processed foods are mostly "empty calories," because, though they have the same energy content per calorie, they lack the vitamins, minerals, antioxidants, phytochemicals, and fiber in plants that are vital to health. So you get more monetary bang for your caloric buck when you eat healthier foods.
3. **Eat at Home.** Dining out can be a weekly treat but perhaps not a daily rite.
4. **Pack Your Lunch.** It may not be possible every day, but if you want to save money, make it a rule rather than an exception.

5. **Buy in Bulk.** Find grocery stores and natural food stores that feature bins of dried beans, pasta, grains, and flour. They are much less expensive because you're not paying for packaging and brand advertising.
6. **Cook from Scratch.** Of course there are times you just want to order a pizza, but in the end, cooking from scratch is always healthier and much more affordable than eating out or buying premade convenience foods.
7. **Become a Savvy Shopper.**
   a. Make a list and stick to it.
   b. Look on the lower shelves for less flashy (and thus less expensive) packaging.
   c. Eat before you shop.
   d. Don't browse every aisle.
   e. Put off going to the grocery store even when you think you have "nothing" in the house. Most likely, you have enough to make a few more meals before heading to the store.

We pay very high costs for cheap animal products—costs to our health, costs to the Earth, and certainly huge costs paid by the animals themselves.

Eating plant-based is the solution; don't let anyone tell you it's the problem.

Week 36

Avoid Animal Cruelty When Traveling

There has been a noticeable increase in the popularity of animal attractions in recent years, whether due to a desire for unique and immersive experiences, the influence of social media in showcasing such encounters, or the expansion of travel opportunities to destinations offering these attractions. As more and more opportunistic operators take advantage of the public's desire to be close to animals—to ride them, swim with them, or get a photo taken with them—more and more animals are suffering. If we're truly enamored with animals, the best way we can demonstrate our affection for them is to leave them alone, especially wild animals. (See Week 12: Embrace Ethical Entertainment.)

There is absolutely no way to have a personal, up-close experience with a wild animal without causing them harm. Wild animals—whether they're in water or on land—want *zero* interaction with humans, and if they're having it in any way, you can be 100 percent certain that cruelty is involved. There is no other way to make wild animals submissive enough to interact with human beings than to break them—beat them, starve them, terrify them.

For every captive or trained animal you pay to see within any kind of tourist trade, you can be sure that entire families were killed. Tourists are especially vulnerable because they want to have what is marketed as a "rich" and "unique" cultural experience, such as

- bullfights in Spain and Mexico;
- horse-driven carriage rides in US and European cities;
- rodeos in the Southern and Western United States;
- swimming with dolphins, feeding stingrays, or holding sea turtles for photo ops in the Caribbean or Mexico;
- elephant rides in Thailand.

We even associate animal-based "delicacies" with certain countries, but you don't need to eat foie gras to enjoy France, haggis to enjoy Scotland, or hamburgers to enjoy the United States. No country has a monopoly on animal exploitation, and it would be insulting to suggest that these countries are defined only by these specific types of cruelty. But when travelers are the main customers, we need to be mindful, informed, and vigilant in order to avoid exploiting animals—everywhere we go.

As a general rule, if a wild animal is involved in an activity, just avoid it. But here are some specific attractions to say no to:

- NEVER pay to ride an elephant.
- NEVER pay for any entertainment where animals are performing.
- NEVER pay to get your photo taken with *any wild animal*—baby or adult.
- NEVER buy elephant paintings.
- NEVER buy animal-derived trinkets or products such as elephant tusks, ivory, animal skins, or sea turtle shells and eggs.
- NEVER pay to pet or walk any wild animal—especially babies and even if you are told they were orphaned and cannot be released.
- NEVER pay to ride in a horse-drawn carriage.
- AVOID animal stalls in open outdoor markets where exotic species such as iguanas, alligators, and monkeys are sold.
- AVOID exotic animal cafés. Even most cat cafés exist as entertainment for people, not as adoption centers for homeless animals.

Finally, be wary of marketing language that lure well-intentioned tourists into an animal exploitation trap. Those who operate animal attractions know that most people don't *want* to contribute to cruelty, so they use euphemisms that disguise the fact that they are places of exploitation—calling them "sanctuaries," "conservation centers," "orphanages," "parks," "preserves," "refuges," and so on.

Red Flags to Know It's Not a Sanctuary

In Week 12: Embrace Ethical Entertainment, I encouraged you to do your due diligence to make sure that a sanctuary is a true sanctuary—a place of refuge—for animals. And while researching a facility before you visit is always a good first step, here are some red flags to look for to avoid supporting animal cruelty.

- If babies are advertised as a must-see attraction—for petting, cuddling, or photos.

- If riding animals is allowed at all.
- If wild animals are tied up or kept in an enclosure to give humans easy access. (This is different from a true wild animal sanctuary where, while there is still protective fencing to keep them safe, the animals are able to roam freely throughout the property.)
- If animals are made to perform any kind of trick for visitors.
- If any type of goads, such as bullhooks or sticks, are used. (These weapons may not be in plain view to the public, and you may be told they're just there to "guide" the animal and are never used *on* the animal, but you can be certain they use them behind closed doors.)

There's so much we can do to avoid supporting places of cruelty.
- Do your homework before you go.
- Read reviews on travel websites and blogs.
- Spread the word to friends, family, and social media followers.
- Learn the difference between animal attractions and true conservation programs, reputable safaris, and ethical animal treks.
- Report photos of people posing with wildlife on social media platforms. Several social media companies collaborate with organizations such as the World Wildlife Fund (WWF), TRAFFIC (Trade Records Analysis of Flora and Fauna in Commerce), and INTERPOL (International Criminal Police Organization) to combat wildlife trafficking.
  › Instagram has implemented content filters and reporting mechanisms to remove and report illegal wildlife trade content.
  › Facebook's artificial intelligence (AI) and machine learning tools help detect and remove illegal wildlife trade content shared on its platforms.
  › YouTube removes illegal wildlife trade content.
  › If you see any such content, report it to the respective platform.

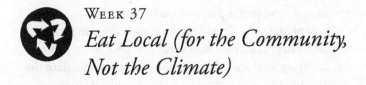

Eat Local (for the Community, Not the Climate)

Every Saturday, my husband and I pack up our empty backpacks and take a 1.5-mile stroll to our local farmers market. Except for a few extras we might need at grocery stores between these weekly trips, 90 percent of the fruits and vegetables we eat at home are grown locally on organic farms.

And for this semimonthly ritual, we may be contributing to more greenhouse gases than if we bought our produce from large-scale, nonorganic producers at supermarkets. That might be a *bit* of an exaggeration, but not much. While there are indeed many evidence-based benefits to supporting local, small-scale farmers, a smaller carbon footprint is *not* one of them.

The premise of the "locavore movement" that began in the early 2000s revolved around the idea of consuming food that is produced within a relatively short distance from where it is consumed—typically within a hundred miles or so. This movement emphasizes supporting local farmers and producers, promoting community resilience, fostering a deeper connection between consumers and their food sources, and reducing the environmental impact of food transportation.

Concerning that last point in particular, the research suggests that *eating locally* may not be as environmentally friendly as initially thought—especially when it comes to curbing greenhouse-gas emissions.

Transportation

The main reason for this is that transportation accounts for only a small portion of greenhouse-gas emissions in agriculture. Furthermore, the transportation methods used in larger systems of import and export—such as ships, trains, or tractor-trailers—tend to produce fewer emissions than the multiple short trips often involved in local food systems.[43] The only small exception is food that has traveled by air—such as highly perishable, shelf-unstable foods like lettuces and fresh berries—but even that accounts for very little of our food footprint.

The other reason is that while the locavore movement encompasses various aspects of local food production—including fruits, vegetables, and artisanal goods—locavores tend to emphasize the consumption of meat, dairy, and eggs from local sources, justifying local animal agriculture as the way to reduce the environmental impact associated with large-scale industrial animal farming.

But as we explored in Week 2: Eat Less Meat, if you want to have the biggest positive environmental impact, it's better to focus on *what* you eat, rather than on *how far* it traveled. This is especially true when it comes to animal products, namely beef, lamb, pork, chicken, and dairy.

Whether meat from animals comes from a nearby farm or is transported from thousands of miles away, it doesn't significantly affect the total emissions of that meat. Why? Because transportation usually contributes less than 1 percent to beef's greenhouse-gas emissions.[44] The carbon footprint of your steak dinner isn't determined primarily by its *origin* but rather by the fact that it's made from beef. Methane emissions, land use, feed production, water use, and processing and packaging are the reasons animal-derived meat has such a negative environmental impact. If reducing your carbon footprint is your aim, you would do better to eliminate animal products from your diet than eat locally sourced meat, dairy, and eggs.

Animal products aside and greenhouse gases notwithstanding, there are indeed reasons to support local produce farms.

Health

While the research doesn't support the claim that locally grown produce is more nutritious than produce with higher food miles, the research does show that people who buy local produce (or grow it themselves) tend to consume a wider *range* of vegetables—and eat more vegetables overall.[45] That's a good thing.

Cost

I'm always surprised when I hear people say they don't shop at their local farmers market because it's more expensive than buying from their grocery store. Personally, I have *never* found this to be the case, and the research bears it out. On average, produce sold directly to consumers is less expensive than that found in grocery stores.[46] One of the reasons for this is that local food systems tend to empower farmers by eliminating intermediaries, allowing them to make a higher profit. Another economic benefit of buying local is the multiplier effect: money spent locally circulates within the community, stimulating additional economic activity.

Food Safety

While larger farms that serve schools or supermarkets are required to have food safety certification, most smaller direct-to-consumer farmers are not. The high cost of this certification means that many local farmers opt out of it, but that doesn't mean they don't prioritize food safety practices. One of the advantages of engaging with local farms is that you can directly inquire about their food safety practices.

Flavor

Research on whether locally produced produce tastes better than produce grown far away and shipped is mixed. While some studies suggest that locally grown produce tends to have better flavor due to factors such as freshness and ripeness at harvest, other research finds little to no difference in taste between locally sourced and nonlocal produce.

Community

Finally, research indicates that participation in farmers markets, CSAs (community-supported agriculture), or food cooperatives does enhance community engagement, fostering feelings of pride, civic duty, and overall togetherness within the community.[47]

And so, my husband and I will keep visiting our neighborhood farmers market—not because we think it drastically reduces our carbon footprint, but because it aligns with other things that matter to us: supporting local farms, walking to a nearby market, engaging with our community, spending time together, and picking out fresh, beautiful produce.

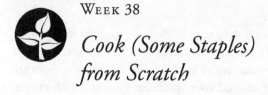

WEEK 38

Cook (Some Staples) from Scratch

Learning to make some kitchen staples from scratch means cutting down on single-use packaging and plastic, saving money, and enjoying the simple joys of homemade goodness. You may not want to make your own ketchup, mayonnaise, nondairy butter, or wine, but plenty of things we buy in the store can easily be made at home.

Here are a few to get you started.

Vegetable Stock: Simmer assorted vegetable scraps (carrot peels, onion ends, celery leaves) with salt, pepper, and preferred herbs in water for 45 minutes (less time if using a pressure cooker)Strain, transfer to jars or containers, and use right away or store in the fridge or freezer for future use.

Nut and Seed Butters: Blend roasted or raw nuts or seeds (almonds, peanuts, sunflower seeds, etc.) in a food processor until smooth. Be patient. At first it may turn into a clump and just turn round and round, but give it a few minutes, and it will soon be a delicious smooth butter! Add salt to taste and store in an airtight container.

Plant-Based Nut Milks: Soak nuts (almonds, peanuts, cashews) overnight. Blend with water (usually a ratio of 4 cups of water to 1 cup of nuts), then strain. Sweeten and add vanilla, if preferred. Refrigerate and use within a few days. (Use the protein-rich leftover pulp to add to muffins or smoothies!)

Basic Balsamic Vinaigrette: Whisk together olive oil, balsamic vinegar, Dijon mustard, and your favorite sweeteners—perhaps a drizzle of maple syrup. Salt and pepper to taste.

Pesto: Blend together until smooth: fresh basil leaves, garlic cloves, pine nuts or walnuts, olive oil, and salt. Or leave out the nuts and call it a pistou!

Cashew-Based Cheeses: Blend until smooth: soaked cashews, lemon juice, nutritional yeast, garlic powder, and salt.

Seitan: Knead 1 cup of dry vital gluten with ½ cup vegetable stock and 2 tablespoons tamari soy sauce. Once a ball is formed, break into smaller balls, and simmer in vegetable stock for 45 minutes. The balls will expand. Let cool, and store in stock in the fridge, or slice and use in recipes.

Quick-Pickled Vegetables: To a large jar, add chopped mixed vegetables (carrots, radishes, cucumbers, red onions, cauliflower, beets). Bring to a boil in a pot white vinegar, apple cider vinegar, water, sugar, salt, and spices and herbs (peppercorns, mustard seeds, cloves, etc.). Pour hot brine over veggies. Let cool, seal, and refrigerate. Enjoy for up to 4 weeks.

Better than Bacon (Carrot, Tofu, or Tempeh): Slice 4 large carrots, 1 block of extra-firm tofu, or 1 package of tempeh (steam it first). Prepare a common marinade by mixing 3 tablespoons of tamari soy sauce, 1 tablespoon maple syrup, 1 tablespoon liquid smoke, 1 teaspoon smoked paprika, and ½ teaspoon garlic powder. Marinate each bacon type for 30 minutes. Heat a pan and fry the marinated slices, each for approximately 5 to 7 minutes per side. Make a BLT!

Corn Tortillas: Combine 2 cups masa harina with 1½ cups warm water and a ½ teaspoon of salt. Divide into balls, press into a thin round. (Use a tortilla press if you have one.) Cook on a hot skillet for 30 seconds each side. Transfer them to a napkin-lined basket to keep warm.

Whatever you make and for whatever reason, savor the satisfaction of saving money, fully controlling flavor and ingredients, and reconnecting with traditional cooking methods.

Week 39

Step Into Compassionate Fashion
Leather without Animal Skins

When I first stopped eating animals—when I became vegetarian—I continued to buy leather and suede (a type of leather made from the underside of animal skins, typically from goats, lambs, or deer). Even though I wasn't eating the flesh of cattle for ethical reasons, I was still wearing their skin, justifying it as an innocent byproduct repurposed from leftover parts on the slaughterhouse floor.

It's going to go to waste anyway, I rationalized; *the harm has already been done.*

It wasn't until I *became vegan* that I stopped eating or wearing anything that came out of or off of an animal—not because I felt I had to be an obedient vegan and follow some sort of rule book, but because I had to acknowledge the inconsistencies in my behavior. When I first became *vegetarian*, I would have said that it was because I didn't want to contribute to a mechanized factory system that treats animals as so many outputs and inputs. Several years later when I became *vegan*, it was because I didn't want to contribute to the inherently violent system that is slaughter. And regardless of what an animal is bred or raised for, the end is always the same, and it's always slaughter. There is no such thing as a slaughter-free animal agriculture system.

As I shared in Week 2: Eat Less Meat, because of resource depletion, pollution, habitat destruction, water use, and greenhouse-gas emissions, raising cattle and sheep is the most environmentally destructive of all types of animal agriculture. In other words, regardless of what the animals are used for once they're dead (meat, leather, wool, gelatin), most of the environmental damage has already occurred—when they were alive. When it comes to leather production, however, the harm continues in the tanning process, which releases toxic chemicals such as chromium, formaldehyde, and ammonia into the environment, contaminating water sources and soil.

Luckily, a growing movement towards cruelty-free and sustainable alternatives is giving the animal leather industry a run for its money.

Synthetic Leather

Synthetic leather, also known as faux leather or vegan leather, has gained traction in the marketplace due to increasing demand for sustainable and cruelty-free alternatives. While there are still environmental impacts (use of chemicals, limited durability, slower decomposition), synthetic leather is generally found to be more eco-friendly than leather made from the skin of cows.[48] And, of course, it's slaughter-free.

As for the health hazards, there are considerations for synthetic as well as animal-skin leather. In synthetic leather production, workers face risks from exposure to chemicals like solvents and plasticizers, which can lead to respiratory issues. In contrast, animal leather tanning poses serious health risks primarily due to the use of toxic chemicals such as chromium salts, particularly hexavalent chromium, a known carcinogen.

Plant Leather

Even better, ethical brands are pioneering innovative materials, such as plant-based leather, that are revolutionizing the fashion industry. Mushroom leather, pineapple leather, and apple leather are all cruelty-free and biodegradable. With advancements in material science and manufacturing processes, plant-based leathers now rival the look, feel, and durability of animal leather, providing consumers with stylish and sustainable options.

Secondhand Leather

A common question I receive is whether or not it is ethical to wear *secondhand* leather or leather shoes, jackets, or purses from our pre-vegan days. Truly, I cannot speak for all vegans—no one can—because there is no single right answer.

But what I can say is that living an examined life means learning to tolerate the gray areas we inevitably encounter. Wearing old leather shoes until they wear out doesn't make us less vegan. It just makes us more human: imperfect humans in an imperfect world.

What I found to be the case for myself and what I think is the case for many is that once you become awake to and aware of animal suffering, you very naturally become less comfortable with animal products in your home and on your person, and so, inevitably, you start to eliminate them from your life—sometimes slowly, sometimes right away. It depends. There's no one answer.

It's all part of the process.

What I have also found is that *if* and *as* you're able to afford replacing these items, you *can* and *will*.

If you still feel guilty about keeping items with animal products on them, I invite you to ask yourself a few questions:

- How does *keeping* this leather couch, these leather shoes, purses, or jackets contribute to animal cruelty right now?

Or flipped around:

- How would getting rid of these items *help* animals right now?

The answer to these questions may help you decide what to do next, or at least enable you to forgive yourself and alleviate any guilt you might be feeling.

As for buying leather from secondhand stores, that's also up to the comfort level of each individual. But rest assured: unlike buying new leather, buying secondhand leather absolutely does not support the leather industry in any way, and it does not create any demand for new ones to be made. The damage has already been done. The supply–demand loop is closed.

Living compassionately is a journey of a hundred miles, a thousand mistakes, and a million lessons. There is no one right way to do what's right. You just put your best foot forward and let compassion guide you.

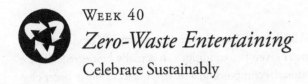

Zero-Waste Entertaining
Celebrate Sustainably

While many of us diligently implement eco-friendly practices in our day-to-day routines, it may feel like a struggle to do the same when organizing an event—whether we're hosting an elegant dinner party indoors or a summer soirée outside. With a little forethought and a few easy swaps, we can absolutely entertain while still having the lightest footprint possible.

Let's begin at the beginning: the decision to do so.

Aspiring to live *zero waste* is not always easy, and it's never perfect. Unfortunately, it's so much more *convenient* to be wasteful, but by virtue of you reading this book, my guess is that convenience is not what you're after. Compassion is. Still, here are some fun and easy ways to host a sustainable celebration without adding too much stress.

Invitations

The most environmentally friendly choice is to use digital invitations, but if you are committed to sending invitations through the mail, check out *seed paper* stationery; it's special paper that contains flower seeds, which guests can then plant or pot with some soil once they're home.

Decorations

- If your party is outdoors, let nature be your decorator. Utilize natural features like flowers, leaves, pine cones, and branches for simple, eco-friendly adornments.
- Ditch the balloons, a serious environmental hazard, and choose reusable items that can be repurposed.
- Use a chalkboard or reusable slate to create signs and labels for different areas of the party.
- Create or buy an eco-friendly banner. With recycled paper letters, some string, and a hole-punch, I have used the same banner for multiple occasions, changing the message ("HAPPY BIRTHDAY," "WELCOME," "CONGRATULATIONS") to suit the need.

Tableware

Plates, cutlery, and napkins labeled "certified compostable" or "biodegradable" mean nothing if they aren't given the conditions to actually biodegrade. These items tend to require industrial composting, a service not available in every city. If you do have that option, great! Add them to the compost! If not, just remember that disposing of "biodegradable" serveware in regular waste bins means they'll probably end up in a landfill where they don't break down. Depending on the occasion and size of the group, consider using ceramic dishware or china—from your own cupboards, borrowed from friends, or bought from a thrift shop. Rent if you need extras. And keep in mind that "reusables" doesn't have to mean "breakables"; see if you can borrow or find reusable *plastic* or *bamboo* plates and cutlery for outdoor parties.

Tablescape

Create centerpieces using trimmed or fallen branches and leaves, fresh-cut flowers, potted plants, or bowls of seasonal fruit such as lemons, limes, oranges, apples, pears, or pomegranates. Opt for reusable tablecloths, placemats, and napkins.

Food

- A plant-based menu is the most environmentally friendly.
- Serve snacks you find in bulk bins, such as nuts and seeds, dried fruit, trail mix with chocolate chips.
- Instead of buying bags of popcorn, make popcorn at home and season with delicious herbs and spices.
- Instead of buying bags of potato chips, make kale chips—pull kale leaves away from the tough stem, tear the leaves into pieces, toss with some oil and salt, place on a baking sheet, and bake in a 350-degree oven for 10 minutes or until crisp. (An air fryer speeds this process up immensely.)

Beverages

- Serve drinks in reusable glasses, and ask everyone to mark their glasses with "glass charms" or a temporary glass marker. That way everyone knows whose glass is whose.
- Rather than provide single-use bottles or cans, serve homemade large-batch drinks, such as fruit- or herb-infused water, lemonade, iced tea, or sangria. Consider renting a pony keg from a local brewery.

- To make carbonated beverages, borrow a SodaStream machine.
- For store-bought soda, beer, or wine, opt for glass bottles or aluminum cans rather than plastic.

Gifts and Party Favors

Sustainable gift-giving doesn't mean never buying anything physical; it means buying something your recipient will value, use, and keep. One of my favorite aspects of traveling is thoughtfully choosing special items for specific friends and family members wherever I am in the world. When I arrive back home, I add them to a *gift drawer* I have in my nightstand, then dole them out during special occasions, holidays, or birthdays. However, of course, there are zero-waste gift options that don't involve giving a physical item:

- Consider giving experiences such as gift certificates to cooking classes or tickets to events, concerts, plays, and performances.
- Give digital gifts such as e-books or homemade gifts such as cookies.
- Make a donation in the recipient's name to an animal or environmental organization.

Disposal and Cleanup

- Set up clearly labeled compost and recycling bins to ensure proper disposal.
- Empty the dishwasher before guests arrive. Ask friends to scrape food waste into the compost bin and place the rinsed dishes in the dishwasher when they're done eating. (Dishwashers use much less water than washing dishes by hand.)

Leftovers: If you do end up with leftovers, donate extras to local organizations, or offer a flash giveaway on your local Buy Nothing group.

Waste Audit: Conduct a waste audit after the event to assess areas for improvement in waste reduction. Because, no doubt, it will not have been perfect. But doing something is better than doing nothing!

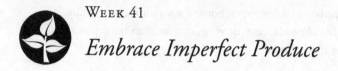

Embrace Imperfect Produce

Did you know that thousands of pounds of perfectly edible fruits and vegetables get thrown in the trash because of arbitrary standards for appearance, shape, and color set by grocery stores—because they're either too small, too large, too mis-shapen, or too "cosmetically challenged"? While restaurants and supermarkets are responsible for 40 percent of food waste in the United States, individual households contribute 43 percent of discarded food—that's 60 million tons of food every year.[49]

While some of this is due to improper storage (see Week 13), a misunder-standing of "sell by" labels (see Week 22), an aversion to leftovers (see Week 25), and intentionally dumping food rather than properly composting it, some of it is simply because of beauty bias!

Thus, it's worth looking at how favoring "perfect" produce in our own homes also leads to food trash:

- When we discard an entire head of lettuce because the outer leaves are slightly wilted (though the inner leaves are perfectly fine).
- When we toss out celery stalks that have brown spots, garlic bulbs that have green sprouts, and carrots that are slightly limp.
- When we throw away bananas that have become "too ripe"—too brown, mushy, and soft. (Sacrilege, in my house!)

There's nothing wrong with wanting perfectly plump plums or temptingly tender figs. Produce that is fat, fleshy, and brightly colored is indeed a testament to its ripeness and a clue to its succulence, but it's worth saying that browning celery, sprouting garlic, or softening carrots can still be eaten.

Rehydrate

Browning is a sign of oxidation, and produce that looks a bit dry and shriveled is simply thirsty. Both are natural processes that can be slowed down in order to prolong the life and appearance of fruits and vegetables. How? By reintroducing them to moisture. A little water does wonders for plumping up produce that has become a little bendy. For instance:

- Celery, carrots, and chopped potatoes will perk up if placed in a bowl of water.
- Wilted spinach and limp asparagus can be revived if placed upright in a glass of water.
- For floppy broccoli or cauliflower, cut the heads into florets and place them in a bowl of water.
- For fresh herbs, trim the stalk bottoms and place upright in a glass of water, or freeze them using the instructions in Week 50: Prolong Shelf Life.

Reserve

While it's natural for fruits and vegetables to start breaking down at some point, prolonging their shelf life really comes down to how they're stored. Here are a few general things to keep in mind:

1. Wash produce just before you eat it—not before you store it.
2. If you *do* wash fruits and veggies prior to putting them in the fridge, be sure to dry them thoroughly.
3. If your refrigerator has a crisper / fruit drawer, *use* it. The lower humidity setting lets out some of the ethylene gases (which speeds up the ripening process).
4. See Week 25: Eat Leftovers for more.

Repurpose

No matter how diligent you are, some produce will inevitably pass its prime and lose its appeal, but that's still no reason to toss it. Converting tired-looking fruits and veggies into a more edible—or potable—form is a creative, responsible way to ensure food consumption rather than food dumping:

- Make vegetable stock with limp veggies.
- Make pie, cobbler, or cake with tired-looking apples, pears, peaches, or persimmons.
- Make applesauce from older apples.

- In fact, use anything—fresh or flimsy—to make some kind of baked good—carrots for cake, blueberries for muffins, ripe bananas for bread.
- Peel and break up very ripe bananas, add the chunks to an airtight container, then store in the freezer for "nice cream" or smoothies anytime.
- Turn lemons into lemonade (literally) or oranges or pomegranates into juice. Store in either the fridge or freezer.
- Before you juice any citrus fruit, zest it first! Whether it's a lemon, lime, or orange, use a zester or microplane to zest the outer rind, then either use the zest right away or store it in the fridge or freezer.
- Pickle! You can pickle almost any fruit or veggie from peppers, beets, onions, and cauliflower to fennel, garlic, cucumbers, even watermelon rinds!
- Turn whole fruits into jams, jellies, preserves, or marmalades; even simpler: turn them into chutney or compote.
- Convert fresh tomatoes into tomato sauce or tomato paste.
- Transform apples into juice, vinegar, or hard cider, aka "apple jack."

The point is, any produce that is no longer at its peak still has use, still has value, still has life—just in another form.

Reach Out

The USDA has created a goal to cut American food waste by 50 percent by 2030, which is achievable if food producers, distributors, retailers, *and* consumers all do their part. Governments are also stepping up—restricting or prohibiting the disposal of organic material into landfills, facilitating food donation programs between restaurants/supermarkets and food banks, providing funding for the development of composting facilities—so reach out to your local or state legislators to find out whom you can support and what you can do to help.

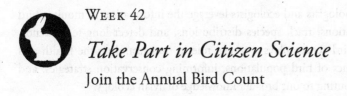

Take Part in Citizen Science

Join the Annual Bird Count

Forget counting sheep! Count chickadees, and make a difference!

Every winter, bird enthusiasts across the globe unite for a shared purpose: the annual bird count. This event, known as the Christmas Bird Count (CBC), has become a cherished tradition and a cornerstone of citizen science, engaging people of all ages and backgrounds in observing and documenting avian populations.

The roots of the Christmas Bird Count trace back to the late nineteenth century. In 1900, ornithologist Frank M. Chapman proposed an alternative to the then-popular "side hunt," a competitive event where teams would compete to shoot the greatest number of birds. Chapman suggested a new tradition—a Christmas bird *census*—aimed at promoting bird conservation. The first official CBC took place on Christmas Day in 1900, with twenty-seven observers counting birds in twenty-five locations across North America.

Over the decades, the Christmas Bird Count has evolved into a massive collaborative effort. Administered by the National Audubon Society, it now spans more than 2,600 locations in the Western Hemisphere, involving tens of thousands of volunteers. The count typically occurs within a designated fifteen-mile diameter circle, and participants spend one full day tallying every bird species they encounter.

For those eager to get involved, simply visit the official Christmas Bird Count website to find a count near you. Local coordinators organize the counts, and participants can join as individuals or teams. The CBC welcomes all skill levels, making it an excellent opportunity for beginners to learn from seasoned birders.

On the chosen day, volunteers head to their designated areas, armed with binoculars and bird guides. Every bird sighted and identified is recorded, contributing to a comprehensive snapshot of the local birdlife. The data collected during these counts have a lasting impact, aiding ongoing research and conservation efforts:

- Ornithologists and ecologists leverage the information to monitor bird populations, track species distributions, and detect long-term trends. This bird census plays a crucial role in understanding the health and dynamics of bird populations, informing conservation strategies, and contributing to our broader knowledge of avian ecology.
- As climate change continues to impact ecosystems, the Christmas Bird Count also serves as a sentinel for ecological shifts. Birds are highly responsive to environmental changes, and shifts in their distribution or abundance can signal broader transformations in habitats. The long-term nature of the CBC provides a unique lens through which researchers can investigate the ecological consequences of climate change.

Beyond its scientific significance, the Christmas Bird Count fosters a sense of community and environmental stewardship. Participants often share their passion for birds, exchanging knowledge and experiences during the count. The event encourages a deeper connection between people and the natural world, emphasizing the importance of biodiversity conservation. It's an opportunity to witness the beauty of winter birdlife, appreciate the diversity of species, and contribute to a global effort that spans generations.

If you want to conduct your own personal bird count—and bird identification—in your own backyard or wherever you are, there are many apps you can download on your phone. My favorite is called Merlin, developed by the Cornell Lab of Ornithology, which provides stellar photo and sound identification. You can build your own list based on what types of birds you hear and see, and the database provides detailed information about each one.

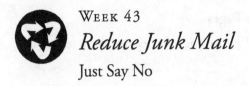

WEEK 43
Reduce Junk Mail
Just Say No

People often ask me what I have found to be the biggest culprit hindering the "zero" part of my zero-waste journey, and my answer is *mail*—junk mail, promotional flyers, catalogs, credit card offers, charity solicitations, local business advertisements, political campaign materials, even the occasional phone book (archaic though it is).

Our mailing addresses and email addresses—considered among the most valuable commodities for both for-profit businesses and nonprofit organizations—are bought and sold often without our awareness or our permission. Direct mail marketing in the United States is a multibillion-dollar industry and results in billions of pieces of junk mail in our mailboxes every year, most of which is made from virgin paper and almost half of which is sent to landfills unopened.

My definition of waste ("any item for which its owner has stopped taking responsibility") and my definition of *zero* waste ("bringing only those things into our lives that we can use and value") compelled me to cauterize the flow of physical mail into my mailbox—even though I never asked for most of it in the first place, at least not intentionally. It took time and vigilance, but I can absolutely attest to a huge decrease in the amount of unsolicited mail we receive at home. Here are some of the steps you can take.

Credit Card Offers

1. Call 1-888-5-OPTOUT (567-8688) or visit optoutprescreen.com to opt out of credit bureaus such as Equifax, Trans Union, and Experian selling your information to banks and credit card companies. You can choose to opt out for five years or permanently; be sure to take these steps for each person in your household.
2. For credit cards you have a relationship with, request that they include you on their "in-house" list, which is not shared or sold to other companies.

Telephone Books and Yellow Pages

Opt out of telephone books and yellow pages by registering at yellowpages optout.com.

Regular Bills

Switch to paperless bills by logging into the accounts for various companies whose services you use—water, gas, electric, phone, house alarm, bank, waste management, etc. (*NOTE*: Check the privacy preferences for these companies. For instance, by default, banks often share your information with other financial institutions. Opt out of any information sharing and marketing communications when you have the option.)

Magazine and Newspaper Subscriptions

Some magazines and newspapers have digital versions available to read on your phone or tablet.

Charity Mailings

Most nonprofits don't use national databases, so you will want to contact each charity you receive solicitations from and ask to be removed from their mailing list—and to not sell your information to others. While many organizations, particularly environmental ones, tend to use recycled or FSC-certified paper for their solicitations, you can pick and choose which charities you want to receive physical mail from versus email. Give them a call, and ask for the option you prefer.

Catalogs

1. Visit dmachoice.org to remove yourself from various types of mailing lists, including email lists. There is a small fee to do so, and it can take up to ninety days for the flow to stop, but it's worth it. This is also a helpful resource for removing the name and address of a deceased family member.
2. A free alternative is catalogchoice.org, but it only allows you to unsubscribe from catalogs one at a time. Also, Catalog Choice won't unsubscribe you from catalogs that you've been a customer of—only ones you're a "prospect" for. If you've actually purchased something from a company, you'll have to visit their website or call to unsubscribe from future catalogs.

Junk Mail and Promotion Mailers

For Val-Pak coupons, send your request to the address printed on the blue envelope you receive. You can also remove your address from their website: www.val-pak.com/coupons/show/mailinglistsuppression. Have the mailing label handy and fill in your information exactly as it is printed.

Mail sent to "Resident," "Current Resident," or "Current Occupant" can be *refused* or *returned* if it is sent First Class. When unsolicited promotional mail winds up in your mailbox, just write "Return to Sender" on the envelope, and pop it back in the mailbox. By law, the post office must return it to the sender. Alternatively, recycle or compost that piece of mail and call and tell the company to remove you from their list.

While taking these steps may not eliminate junk mail from your mailbox 100 percent of the time, it will make a huge dent and save some trees in the meantime.

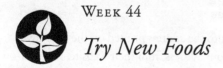

Try New Foods

If you've been eating the same foods, going to the same restaurants, ordering the same menu items, and sticking to the same cuisines all your life (and most of us do), you're most likely stuck in some food ruts. There's nothing wrong with rotating the same familiar meals again and again and finding comfort in them, but expanding our palates and repertoires not only keeps things exciting, it also provides us with an abundance of nutrients we wouldn't otherwise consume.

The good news is that there are thousands of edible plants out there (we probably eat only a few hundred in our lifetimes), so let's start exploring flavors with herbs and spices, which most everyone has in their cupboards but which are typically underutilized.

Herbs and Spices

First and foremost, check your spices and herbs for freshness, and replace what is stale. If there are spices and herbs you use frequently, by all means, keep using them, but try some that are new to you. Here are a few recommendations:

- Tarragon is an underappreciated herb that pairs beautifully with potatoes, asparagus, peas, and mushrooms.
- Sumac, commonly used in Middle Eastern cuisine, is known for its bright, tangy, citrusy flavor. Add it to salads, grains, and roasted vegetables.
- Coriander and cumin seeds pair well with curry and rice dishes, roasted chickpeas, and Indian-inspired vegetable stir-fries.
- Add smoked paprika to bean-based dishes, grilled vegetables, and plant-based paella.
- Fresh herbs (any of them!) instantly elevate green salads.

Vegetables

As I discuss in Week 5: Eat by Color, I recommend exploring the kaleidoscope of colors in plant foods. Walk around the farmers market or produce section of your favorite grocery store and let your eyes guide you. Grab a couple of unfamiliar vegetables and search for recipes online. Another way to explore unfamiliar vegetables is to subscribe to a CSA (Community Supported Agriculture), which delivers locally sourced, seasonal produce directly to your doorstep. Each box is a surprise and will no doubt contain some veggies that are unfamiliar to you.

Grains

I don't know about you, but the rice that was served in my house when I was growing up was *white rice*, "Minute Rice," completely stripped of fiber and devoid of flavor. But that was all I knew. When I began looking outside my comfort zone, a world of grains opened up.

Explore for yourself and bring home some new grains:

- **Brown Rice:** If you're accustomed to white rice, transitioning to brown rice may take some adjustment due to its chewier texture and nuttier flavor. One idea for transitioning would be to mix both types together to get used to the heartier profile of brown rice.
- **Quinoa:** Finally having its day, quinoa is worth all the hype. Protein-packed and fast-cooking, it makes a fantastic base for grain salads, curries, or stir-fries.
- **Barley or Farro:** Both are hearty grains that make for filling, fiber-rich salads and soups. Add mushrooms and greens for added flavor and nutrition.
- **Bulgur:** The most common way to use this light grain is to make tabbouleh salad with finely chopped veggies, olive oil, and lemon juice. Like quinoa, it is very quick-cooking, though it's more accurate to say *quick-soaking*. Just pour boiling water over dried bulgur and let it sit for 20 minutes, until it is tender. Drain, fluff, and season.
- **Buckwheat:** Considered a complete protein because it contains all of the essential amino acids (see Week 23: Build Muscle. Don't Eat It.), buckwheat can be enjoyed in various ways, such as in porridge, pancakes, salads, and stir-fries, offering a nutty flavor and versatile texture as a substitute for oatmeal.

"Vegan" Foods

Of course, ALL plant foods are available to ALL people, but some foods have become so associated with vegans and plant-based eating that it's worth taking a few moments to focus on them. Besides, some may be completely new to you.

- **Tofu,** a versatile soy-based delicacy originating from China, offers textures ranging from silky to firm, allowing you to create velvety puddings, creamy salads, crispy patties, or chewy nuggets.
- **Tempeh,** with its nutty flavor and hearty texture, hails from Indonesia and can be used to make mayo-tossed salads, tempeh bacon, or as the main protein in a stir-fry.
- **Seitan,** a protein-rich plant-based meat crafted from wheat gluten and originating in China, provides a chewy, meaty texture that can replace animal meat in any dish.
- **Nutritional yeast is a flaky,** cheesy delight perfect for making cheese sauces, flavoring (and coloring) tofu scrambles, and seasoning popcorn.

While there's comfort in the familiar, it can be restrictive if *comfort* becomes a *crutch*. Wherever you are on your journey, whether you're vegan or not, now is the perfect moment to broaden your culinary horizons and discover the diverse world of flavors waiting to be explored.

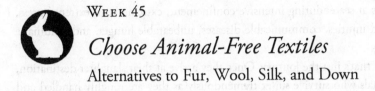

Choose Animal-Free Textiles

Alternatives to Fur, Wool, Silk, and Down

When someone I meet learns that I'm vegan, invariably they take the measure of how "strict" I am by asking with incredulity, "You don't even wear wool? What's wrong with wool?! It's just giving sheep a haircut!" Technically speaking, you don't have to *kill* sheep to make a wool hat, *slaughter* goats to make a cashmere scarf, or *butcher* rabbits to make an angora sweater, but practically speaking, you *do*.

Wool, Cashmere, and Angora

Some breeds of sheep are raised specifically for human consumption, though the consumption of lamb or mutton has been on the decline in recent years. Other breeds of sheep are bred specifically for their hair, for which they are sheared annually for several years, then sent to slaughter when they are no longer *productive*—i.e., when their wool production declines and they become less economically viable.

There is no such thing as a slaughter-free animal agriculture system.

The wool trade is just that: a business meant to maximize profits and minimize losses. As sheep age, their wool production declines, and as a result, ranchers slaughter lower-production animals and replace them with younger, higher-production animals. Similarly, in the cashmere industry, goat breeds not raised specifically for their flesh are bred and used for their soft undercoat, which is sheared to obtain cashmere fibers. Like sheep in the wool industry, cashmere goats are eventually slaughtered once they are deemed no longer suitable for fiber production.

But it's worth saying that the majority of these animals are not slaughtered by the ranchers themselves. They are shipped to other countries—primarily to the Middle East and North Africa—for slaughter, sale, and consumption. Despite years of public opposition and widespread calls to end live animal export, countries such as Australia and New Zealand continue to maintain a prominent role in what is in fact an animal welfare atrocity. Animals are subjected to three to six weeks at sea enduring intensive confinement, extreme heat, extreme stress, untreated injuries, communicable diseases, unbearable hunger, and inhumane handling.

And that's just the journey. Once they arrive at their slaughter destination, the animals who survive suffer tremendously as they are roughly handled and inhumanely killed. "Humane slaughter" laws are weak or nonexistent in the majority of the countries the animals are sold to.

Down and Feathers

The news isn't much better for the ducks and geese kept and killed for their down and feathers. While some are collected as a byproduct of the meat industry, the majority come from birds raised specifically for their feathers. These birds often endure cruel conditions on factory farms, including overcrowded cages, painful debeaking, and rough handling. The live-plucking of feathers from birds without the use of pain relief or anesthesia is also a common practice, resulting in immense suffering and distress.

Eventually, when the birds are no longer considered profitable for feather and down production or when their production declines, they are slaughtered for meat. In some cases, geese and ducks raised for their feathers may also be subjected to force-feeding to produce foie gras, which is made from the enlarged livers of fattened waterfowl. This process, known as *gavage*, involves force-feeding birds large amounts of food to induce rapid weight gain and liver enlargement.

I cannot say this enough, so I'll say it again: there is no such thing as a slaughter-free animal agriculture system.

Fur

Fur, once considered the epitome of luxury, is now recognized as one of the most inhumane and therefore controversial materials in fashion. The fur industry relies on the slaughter of millions of animals, including foxes, minks, rabbits, and chinchillas, who—before they're killed—live in appalling conditions. Animals on fur farms endure years (if they survive) of confinement, stress, and suffering before meeting a brutal end. They are subjected to cramped cages, poor sanitation, and inhumane killing methods, all in the name of fashion. While demand for fur products has declined in many parts of the world because of the cruelty inherent in the fur trade, it remains a multimillion-dollar industry.

Silk

Prized for its luxurious texture and lustrous sheen, silk is derived from the cocoons of silkworms. Of course I have a great task trying to inspire a sense of compassion for worms, but we can't talk about animal-based textiles without talking about silk, and we can't talk about silk without talking about the tens of billions of worms who are used globally each year for silk production.

The process involves boiling the cocoons and killing the caterpillars inside, raising ethical concerns regarding the treatment of sentient beings, as well as environmental issues associated with the large-scale cultivation of mulberry trees, which leads to deforestation and biodiversity loss, excessive water use, and pesticides that impact vulnerable species.

Compassionate Alternatives

The good news is that, in recent years, the fashion industry has witnessed a growing awareness of the negative consequences of animal-derived materials and is embracing nonanimal textiles instead.

- Natural materials provide a cruelty-free alternative to animal-derived fibers. Organic cotton, bamboo, hemp, and Tencel are all renewable, biodegradable materials that offer versatility and comfort.
- Synthetic materials such as faux fur, viscose, acrylic, polyester, and nylon offer comparable aesthetics and performance without the need for animal exploitation.
- Faux fur, in particular, has seen a surge in popularity in recent years, with advancements in manufacturing techniques resulting in high-quality, realistic alternatives to animal fur.
- PrimaLoft and kapok fibers are already widely used as stuffing for comforters, pillows, mattresses, and life jackets due to their buoyancy and ability to repel water. They are also used as filling for cushions and upholstery.
- There are exciting developments with the rise of cell-based and plant-based materials like apple leather, pineapple leather, mushroom leather, cork, and other sustainable alternatives. Cell-based agriculture is also making strides, creating leather-like materials without the need for livestock, further promoting sustainability in fashion. (See Week 39: Step into Compassionate Fashion.)

As with so many issues discussed throughout this book, there are trade-offs, and we do the best we can. Animal products demand substantial land, water, and feed resources, their production generates significant methane emissions, and animal cruelty and exploitation is inherent. Synthetic materials may be derived from petrochemicals, requiring energy use and fossil fuels; they emit fewer direct greenhouse gases compared to animal products but are not biodegradable and may contribute to microplastic pollution. (See Week 28: Reduce Nonessential Plastic Packaging.) Plant-based textiles are more environmentally friendly than synthetic materials, but require land that displaces forests and habitats; cotton is highly water-intensive and relies on pesticides and fertilizers; and organic cotton crops still use great amounts of water as well as land.

Nothing is perfect, but we have many levers to pull in order to make informed, compassionate purchasing decisions. The fashion industry is no different from any other in that it can and will innovate if and when the public demands it.

WEEK 46

Vote for Animal-Friendly Legislators (or Become One Yourself)

While specific individual actions indeed have an impact on the issues we care about, a significant amount of transformation occurs at the legislative level. A single positive policy change can quickly outweigh the combined behaviors of millions of individuals. Voting for legislators who are committed to sustainable, compassionate policies is vital for systemic change, and we can point to several bipartisan examples of pro-animal, pro-conservation, pro-environment laws that have been enacted over the last century.

- In 1906, Republican President Theodore Roosevelt signed into law the Antiquities Act, paving the way for the National Park System that has left a lasting impact on habitat protection for thousands of species. Roosevelt was an avid hunter.
- In 1964, Democrat President Lyndon B. Johnson—a Texan who ate meat, hunted, and fished—signed the Wilderness Act as well as the Land and Water Conservation Fund, securing the permanent protection of 9.1 million acres across North America and creating the National Wilderness Preservation System. He also signed the Animal Welfare Act into law in 1966, establishing basic standards for the treatment of animals in research, exhibition, and transport.
- In 1970, Republican President Richard Nixon established the Environmental Protection Agency, signing both the Clean Air Act and the Clean Water Act, both of which have significantly reduced air and water pollution and prevented many deaths as a result. Nixon also signed the Marine Mammal Protection Act (MMPA) in 1972. Since its enactment, the MMPA has contributed to the recovery of several marine mammal species, including the gray whale, humpback whale, and California sea lions. Nixon himself was quite indifferent to environmental concerns, and yet he has gone down as one of the most environmentally friendly leaders in history.

- Former British Prime Minister Margaret Thatcher—known for her conservative perspectives and policies—put on the map the issues of ozone layer depletion, acid rain, air pollution, and global warming in the mid-1980s. Together with the help of the Republican US president, Ronald Reagan, Thatcher galvanized international support, resulting in the signing of the Montreal Protocol, which ended the use of ozone-destroying chlorofluorocarbons (CFCs).
- The Hunting Act of 2004, introduced in the UK by Tony Blair's Labour government, prohibits hunting with dogs in England and Wales, marking a significant advancement in animal welfare, especially as it pertains to fox hunting.
- In 2020, Democrat Joe Biden campaigned on an ambitious climate platform, and as president, on August 2, 2022, he signed into law the most comprehensive bipartisan climate legislation in US history: the Infrastructure Investment and Jobs Act, which allocates hundreds of billions of dollars for clean energy, electric vehicles, and public transit expansion.

And we can't forget about how local politics matter.

In 2014, an ordinance banning the use of bullhooks on elephants was proposed to the city council in Oakland, California. Despite strong opposition from Feld Entertainment, the then-owner of Ringling Bros. and Barnum & Bailey Circus, over 100 citizens spoke in favor of the ban, which finally passed after midnight. By March 2015, Ringling decided to remove elephants from their circuses since they could no longer use pain and fear for training—the only way to make these sensitive animals submit to humiliating acts. This humane shift led to a decline in ticket sales, and in May 2017, Ringling Bros. Circus closed for good—a triumph for compassionate individuals and, above all, a victory for animals.

This is a powerful example of how a municipal ordinance led to the closure of a commercial enterprise that had thrived on animal exploitation for 160 years.

In short, civic engagement helps to ensure that animals have a seat at the table in local, state, and national governments. Exercising this democratic privilege is an empowering and effective way of manifesting our compassion, and there are many ways to do so:

1. **Vote.** Voting is just the beginning, but it is an essential beginning. Vote locally, regionally, and nationally, but vote. If you've ever doubted the power of voting, all you need to do is look at the history of and struggle

for suffrage in the United States and around the world, because the power of voting can be measured by the efforts to forbid, suppress, limit, and restrict it.

2. **Research candidates' positions on environmental and animal welfare issues before voting.** Consult national organizations that lobby on behalf of animals as well as local PACs (political action committees) for information and endorsements of animal-friendly and environment-friendly candidates.

3. **Contact elected officials to advocate for policies and laws that protect animals and the environment.** Remember, elected officials work for their constituents—not the other way around. They work for *you*, whether you voted for them or not. Worry less about what to say to *them* and focus more on asking them to tell you their position on relevant animal issues.

4. **Make *your* single issue *one* of their many issues.** The roles of government leaders are many, and they vary according to their positions, but one thing is certain: they do not have the luxury of focusing on one single issue. While animal protection may be top of mind for *you*, it may never cross their mind—not because they don't care but because they've never thought about it. You can help them think about it. Especially at the local level, you have the opportunity to establish relationships with city and county administrators and legislators to ensure that animal issues are on their agenda. Presume good intentions, establish contact, and work together on ways to pass legislation that could protect animals.

5. **Send a heartfelt thank-you to legislators when they do vote for legislation you care about.** Legislators have a thankless job; they're continually blamed and criticized, even for things out of their control. Getting a letter of recognition once in a while goes a long way in making them feel appreciated. More than that, one letter of gratitude represents hundreds of unwritten letters and indicates to them what their constituents want to see more of.

6. **Support animal-friendly legislation by campaigning.** This may involve recruiting volunteers, writing letters to legislators, writing op-eds to newspapers, organizing phone banks, knocking on doors, and engaging in other grassroots organizing activities to build support and mobilize public pressure on elected officials for animal-friendly initiatives.

7. **Stay informed and engaged by following reputable, independent news sources.** An informed citizen is an empowered citizen. Reading

incendiary news headlines and sensational social media posts does not constitute civic engagement—neither is it healthy. Prioritize trusted sources and in-depth analysis that provide a balanced perspective of issues and events.

Finally, keep perspective and have hope. Just because we have work to do doesn't mean work hasn't been done. History gives you great perspective if you just look back and take note of all the ways we've progressed as individuals and as a society. If we didn't believe that, none of us would even bother trying to create change, and you wouldn't be reading this book. (See Afterword: Why I'm Hopeful.)

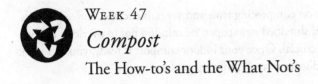

Compost
The How-to's and the What Not's

If you're new to composting, fear not! It's easier than you might think. Before we break it down (no pun intended) into straightforward options that suit different lifestyles, let's break down what it is. Composting is simply the intentional decomposition of organic matter into nutrient-rich soil, requiring a balance of nitrogen ("green" materials) and carbon ("brown" materials).

Think of green matter as the wet components, like kitchen scraps and fresh grass clippings, and brown matter as the dry, such as dried leaves and shredded newspaper. The balance between wet and dry, green and brown, nitrogen and carbon is what ensures proper decomposition (and also prevents odors). In order to foster microbial activity and break down materials efficiently, compost should be *just right*—not too wet or dry. And it should have a pleasant, earthy aroma—not a foul, unpleasant odor.

Backyard Composting

For those with a bit of outdoor space, backyard composting is an excellent option. All you need is a designated bin or an area dedicated to creating a compost pile. Include kitchen scraps like fruit and vegetable skins, coffee grounds, and tea leaves for the "green" portion of your compost, and dry leaves, shredded newspaper, cardboard, toilet paper rolls, and paper towels for the brown portion. The smaller they are, the faster they'll break down.

Accelerate the decomposition process by turning the compost a few times a week with a shovel or pitchfork. If you have a compost *tumbler*, simply give it a spin every other day. Over time, you'll witness the magic of nature as your kitchen and yard waste transform into nutrient-rich compost. This "black gold"—as composters call this material—can then be used to enhance your garden soil—and thus your plants and the beneficial insects who thrive on these plants.

Indoor Composting

Living in a small space doesn't mean you can't compost. Indoor composting options, such as compost bins designed for apartments, make the process manageable and odor-free. Focus on composting fruit and vegetable scraps, coffee grounds, and small amounts of shredded newspaper. Be mindful not to overload the bin, as proper aeration is crucial. Once your indoor compost is ready, you can use it for potted plants or donate it to community gardens.

Vermicomposting

Vermicomposting, or composting with worms, adds nature's little helpers to the decomposition process. A vermicomposting bin, also known as a worm bin, is a compact system that utilizes red worms to break down organic matter. Simply place your chopped-up kitchen scraps in the worm bin along with shredded newspaper, and the worms will happily devour the material, turning it into nutrient-rich castings. Vermicomposting is an excellent option for apartment dwellers or anyone without outdoor space.

NOTE: Some vegans may avoid vermicomposting because it involves animals, while others view it as part of a natural process, acknowledging that worms are already present in their natural habitat. You can decide what is right for you.

Bokashi Composting

Bokashi "composting" is a unique method that allows you to break down your kitchen waste through fermentation. The process uses beneficial microorganisms to ferment the waste rather than decompose it in the traditional sense. In a Bokashi bin, you simply layer kitchen scraps with the Bokashi mixture they provide—a combination of bran and microorganisms. The bin is sealed tightly to create an anaerobic environment, allowing the fermentation process to take place. After a few weeks, the fermented material is either buried in soil or added to a compost pile for further decomposition. *Voilà!*

Curbside Composting

If you don't want to compost yourself, check with your city's waste-management department to see if they offer curbside compost pickup. If it's not available to you, look for community-driven initiatives in your area that offer private/commercial home pickup compost services. This grassroots approach allows you to contribute to composting efforts without managing a compost pile at home.

Interestingly, studies have shown that people who compost or have access to composting systems may actually generate *more* food waste, possibly because they feel less guilty about discarding food. So don't forget to implement the tips provided in Week 25: Eat Leftovers, Week 41: Embrace Imperfect Produce, Week 50: Prolong Shelf Life, and other chapters to reduce food waste in the first place.

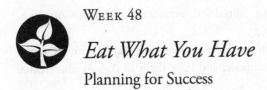

WEEK 48

Eat What You Have

Planning for Success

One of the reasons we let food sit in the fridge without eating it is lack of *planning*. Most of us decide what we're going to eat once we're already hungry, and at that stage, we tend to make decisions based on haste—on how quickly we can fill our empty bellies—not on how well we want to eat.

It might be another story if you follow my advice from Week 8 and already have vegetables chopped up in the refrigerator, but that only strengthens my point: *plan in advance*. This doesn't even require *doing* anything to start. It just requires *thinking*. When it comes to dinner especially, a good rule of thumb is to know the *night before* what you're going to have for dinner the following night. Stretch your planning to the next morning at the very latest, but knowing what you're eating for dinner long before dinnertime arrives increases the likelihood that you will *eat* the perishables in your fridge—and that you will make healthier choices.

Personally, I'm someone who doesn't work well with a *rigid* food schedule—i.e., having dinners planned out Monday through Friday. But I'm also someone who doesn't make last-minute decisions about what I'm going to eat or cook for my family. There are lots of ways to plan ahead while still being flexible. Here are some ideas:

- Whatever you're making for dinner, double it. Eat half of it that night, and refrigerate or freeze the second half for leftovers.
- If you don't already have veggies chopped up in the fridge (see Week 8), before you start your day:
  › take ten minutes to dice up a few carrots, an onion, and a couple of potatoes, and you've got the makings of a soup;
  › chop up an onion and a couple of bell peppers, and you've got chili in your near future;
  › cut up some lettuce, cauliflower, and celery, and a salad is on the horizon.

- If you decide you want a grain dish *tomorrow* night, cook up some rice, quinoa, or barley *tonight*.
- Before you start work in the morning, marinate your favorite vegetables or tofu in a favorite marinade, and leave them all day. At dinnertime, roast or grill them.
- Before you leave for work, remove some jars of homemade veggie stock from the freezer and thaw them on the counter. When you arrive home, you've already got the base for a soup, stir-fry, or risotto. (See Week 38: Cook from Scratch for a quick vegetable stock recipe.
- Before you get dressed in the morning, throw lentils, spices, chopped onions, and garlic into a slow cooker, and turn the heat to low. Come home to enjoy a scrumptious, delicious dinner of Indian dal.
- Buy or borrow a pressure cooker or slow cooker if you don't already have one. They're game-changers when it comes to cooking efficiently and healthfully.

Another way to plan in advance is to create a rough meal schedule for the week based on what you *already have in the house*. This is key. Change the question from "what do I *want* for dinner (or lunch or breakfast)?" to "what do I *have* for dinner (or lunch or breakfast)?"

So, open your fridge, look in the freezer, open your cupboards, and use some ingenuity—or a favorite cookbook—to concoct a fabulous meal from what is already waiting to be used. In other words, put off going to the grocery store for a couple of days and eat up what you already have! This will not only save you money, inspire creativity, and stretch some comfort zones, it will also undoubtedly prevent food from being wasted.

If we're really honest with ourselves, whenever we say "there's nothing to eat in the house," most likely there's *something to eat in the house*. Whenever we declare that "our cupboards are bare," most likely they're quite well stocked, so take inventory. I suspect you will be surprised by how much you can make with what is already in the house.

- Canned beans? Make a casserole, chili, or salad.
- Boxes of pasta? Jars of tomato sauce? Whip up some *spaghetti alla marinara* or *pasta al pomodoro*.
- Bags of flour? Make some waffles, pancakes, biscuits, or bread.
- Brown rice? Make a pilaf, stir-fry, or fried rice.

- Miso paste? Make a simple soup, or use it to make a delicious salad dressing you can use all week.
- Canned tomatoes? Make tomato soup or homemade pasta or pizza sauce.
- Cocoa powder, sugar, flour, and baking powder sitting in the pantry? Bake a cake!
- Overripe or frozen bananas? Make a smoothie or banana muffins.
- Canned cranberry sauce you didn't use last Thanksgiving? Serve it as a side dish tonight.
- Oats? Make overnight oats for tomorrow's breakfast.
- Canned pumpkin purée sitting around? Make a pie! You don't have to wait for the autumn holidays to do so.

The options are endless, and you're limited only by your imagination and will.

Volunteer for Animals

Given the myriad challenges animals face in the world, there is no dearth of opportunities to help. About 50,000 animal organizations are registered as non-profits in the United States, ranging from shelters and welfare organizations supporting domesticated animals to sanctuaries, refuges, and conservation organizations protecting wildlife.[50]

Most of them rely on volunteers to fulfill their mission, and it's not just the animals themselves who benefit. Numerous studies demonstrate the link between helping others and improvements in mental, emotional, and physical health. Allan Luks, author of *The Healing Power of Doing Good*, looked at the well-being of thousands of Americans regularly engaged in volunteer activities and found that they generally exhibited better health, increased enthusiasm, and higher energy levels compared to individuals of the same age who don't volunteer.

These benefits are also apparent whether the recipients are human animals or nonhuman animals. Studies consistently show that taking care of animals contributes to improved psychological and physical health—reducing stress, lowering blood pressure, alleviating anxiety, helping to mitigate symptoms of depression, and potentially increasing longevity. Notable benefits are observed among people who already tend to be isolated, such as the elderly in retirement homes or incarcerated prisoners. Connecting with animals offers the companionship and unconditional love they may be lacking, which creates a sense of purpose and fulfillment.

I'm often asked what type of animal advocacy I think is the most effective. I think a better question to ask is: "What type of advocacy is right for *me*?" Consider your skills, strengths, passions, and what truly inspires you. It might be communication, education, technology, or legislation. It might be cooking, writing, teaching, or building coalitions. Start with what you're most moved by, where you think you would have the most impact, and what you think you would enjoy most. Your own satisfaction counts for a lot. The more gratification you get out of what you're doing, the more enduring and effective your activism will be.

I also think volunteering locally is a good place to start. Reach out to organizations near you to find out what kind of help they need. Whatever road you go down, you can always change your mind and try something else. The options for volunteering are endless.

Ways to Volunteer for Animals

- **Local Animal Shelters:** Municipal shelters run on a very limited budget and rely on volunteers to walk dogs, clean enclosures, socialize cats, photograph adoptable animals, and participate in adoption events.
- **Fostering** (Week 18): This chapter is dedicated specifically to inspiring you to foster dogs, cats, and other homeless animals. Providing a safe, loving transitional space until they find their forever home is one of the most impactful things you can do to help local animals.
- **Animal Therapy:** Enroll your own companion animal in a therapy training program to provide comfort and companionship to individuals in hospitals, nursing homes, schools, prisons, youth detention centers, or other institutions.
- **Community Cats:** Help care for feral and stray cats through activities such as trap-neuter-return (TNR), feeding colonies, providing shelter, and socializing kittens for adoption.
- **Veterinary Clinics:** Volunteer at veterinary clinics, especially those that offer services to low-income populations. Assist with administrative tasks, provide transportation to people or their pets, offer support during spay-neuter clinics.
- **Wildlife Rehabilitation Centers:** Assist in the hands-on care and rehabilitation of injured or orphaned animals and play a crucial role in their return to their wild home.
- **Marine Conservation Projects:** Participate in beach cleanups, coral reef monitoring, and sea turtle nesting surveys. If these opportunities aren't available to you where you live, consider reaching out to marine conservation organizations on your next beach vacation.
- **Wildlife Surveys and Monitoring:** Reach out to local wildlife organizations to participate in surveys and monitoring projects, or collect crucial data on animal populations, behaviors, and habitats. (See Week 42: Join the Annual Bird Count.)
- **Animal Transport:** Whether you do the driving yourself or coordinate the transportation logistics, a crucial piece of animal rescue is transporting

animals to shelters, rescue organizations, foster homes, adopters, veterinary appointments, or wildlife rescue centers.

- **Farmed Animal Sanctuaries:** Reach out to sanctuaries that provide a safe haven for animals rescued from animal factories, research laboratories, and slaughterhouses. There are many around the world. Not all of the jobs are glamorous—mucking barns and fixing fences are constant needs—and aside from hands-on interactions with the animals in their care, you can also help by managing their social media accounts, PR, or fundraising events.

- **Legislation and Lobbying:** This may involve organizing letter-writing campaigns, participating in rallies or protests, lobbying for specific legislation, or creating a political action committee to help elect animal-friendly legislators. (See Week 46: Vote for Animal-Friendly Legislators.)

- **Community Outreach and Education:** This may involve organizing informational events; giving presentations to community groups and schools; using social media to raise awareness about issues affecting animals; leafleting; tabling; or writing articles, op-eds, letters to the editor, or blog posts.

- **Fundraising and Event Planning:** Volunteer to help organize fundraising events, adoption events, or awareness campaigns for animal welfare organizations. This can involve tasks such as event planning, marketing, soliciting donations, and coordinating volunteers.

An added benefit? Your generosity could potentially inspire others. Research consistently affirms that parents engaged in volunteer work are more likely to see their children volunteer when they reach the same age. And children brought up in collectivistic cultures, which prioritize the welfare of the group and community, tend to exhibit greater altruism than those raised in individualistic cultures.

In short, our positive actions create ripple effects beyond what we can even quantify.

Week 50

Prolong Shelf Life

Properly Store Food

From the countertop to the freezer, the way we store our food can significantly influence its freshness, longevity, and ultimately, its fate. Whether it's improper placement in the refrigerator, neglect in the cupboards, or abandonment in the freezer, every decision we make about how we store our food determines whether or not that food will last long enough to be eaten, which is the point of buying food in the first place!

Let's look at the dos and don'ts of food storage and identify some practical strategies to extend the life of our food and curb unnecessary waste.

Refrigerators and Freezers

- Keep refrigerators below 40°F (4°C) and freezers at or below 0°F (-18°C) for optimal preservation.
- Apply the FIFO rule (First In, First Out) to rotate items. When you buy new groceries, move the older items to the front and the new items to the back.
- Regularly check and prioritize eating items close to expiration.
- Avoid overstuffing the fridge; good airflow maintains freshness and also prevents items from getting lost.
- Maintain 75–80 percent freezer capacity for efficient air circulation. If your freezer is filled to the brim, food may block the internal air vents, making it harder for cold air to be distributed throughout the freezer.
- Allow hot foods to cool before transferring them to the fridge or freezer in order to prevent temperature fluctuations.
- Prevent freezer burn by tightly packing food in containers to minimize exposure to air.
- Store dry goods in airtight containers in the refrigerator or freezer. This will not only prolong their freshness, it will also help prevent little critters getting to your food before you do.
- Keep leftovers in clear containers, and don't let them hide in the back.
- Consume leftovers within a week or two.

Freezer Foods

I think people forget that fruits, vegetables, and even herbs can be frozen. Here is a general guide.

How to Freeze Fresh Herbs
- Wash herbs gently and pat them dry thoroughly.
- Finely chop or leave whole.
- Portion into ice cube trays.
- Fill each compartment with water.
- Freeze until solid.
- Transfer to bags, return to freezer, and use within six months.

How to Freeze Fresh Vegetables
- Wash vegetables thoroughly and cut into desired sizes.
- Blanch the vegetables by adding them to boiling water for one minute, then immediately transfer them to an ice bath to stop the cooking process.
- Drain excess water and pat the vegetables dry to prevent ice crystals.
- Place into airtight containers or freezer bags. Label and date.

How to Freeze Fresh Fruit
- Wash, peel, core, and slice/chop, as desired.
- To prevent the chopped fruit from sticking together, freeze them first for a few hours on a baking sheet lined with parchment paper. Once they're frozen, transfer them to a freezer bag or airtight container.

And remember that food in the freezer—especially if well sealed—may last up to six months or more, but the longer something sits in the freezer, the less likely we are to eat it. In general, think of your freezer as short-term rather than long-term storage.

Pantry and Cabinets

While freezing or refrigerating dry goods is a great option if you have the space, most of us store dry goods in cabinets and cupboards, so let's look at how to keep everything from flour, sugar, and baking soda to oats, polenta, and dry pasta from becoming stale or getting eaten by critters.

1. Keep your cupboards and pantry dry, dark, and cool (between 50°F to 70°F)—ideally away from any heat-producing appliances.

2. Place older jars and containers in the front of your cupboards so they get used first.
3. Deter critters by storing dry foods such as rice, sugar, and pasta in dry, airtight containers.

Because flours, especially whole-grain flours, contain fat, when they become rancid it's because the oils in the flours have gone bad. You'll know this has happened when the flour smells off, like old cooking oil. While eating this flour is unlikely to make you sick (small doses of rancid foods generally don't), your baked goods definitely won't taste very good.

Eat Processed Foods (We All Do!)

There are a lot of misconceptions about what it means to be vegan, and I've spent half my life debunking fallacies and falsehoods, especially when it comes to food. Biases against "vegan food" negatively influence public perceptions, and generalizations lead people to dismiss the idea of veganism completely. There is a lot to say about how the word *vegan* can be both a help and a hindrance in the public mind—and I have written a lot about this —but what I want to address here is the common charge that "vegan food" is undesirable because it is *highly processed*.

First of all, I often put "vegan food" in quotation marks, because what falls into that category is regular food that both vegans and non-vegans eat but don't—and shouldn't—call *vegan*: fruits, vegetables, beans, lentils, grains, mushrooms, nuts, seeds, herbs, and spices. We don't say it's a "vegan banana" or a "vegan chickpea." It's just a banana. It's just a chickpea—and therefore it's *suitable for vegans* and non-vegans.

When we stop talking about "vegan food" as if it's a separate food group meant only for vegans, people are more inclined to embrace it. The fact is *everyone* eats fruits, vegetables, beans, lentils, grains, mushrooms, nuts, seeds, herbs, and spices—vegans and non-vegans (though studies show that vegans and vegetarians do eat greater quantities).

Whole plant foods, however, are not on people's minds when they dismiss and disparage "vegan food" for being highly processed. They're talking about vegan *convenience* foods. Pointing to all of the commercially made plant-based burgers, sausages, and nuggets lining grocery store shelves, they conclude that veganism is unhealthy and unsustainable.

Not only is this a straw man argument (just because the products exist doesn't mean you have to eat them), it's also disingenuous (the prepackaged foods industry was a multibillion-dollar sector long before veggie burgers came along). It's also ironic, because it's meat-eaters who have made plant-based meats one of the fastest-growing sectors in the food industry. According to the Good

Food Institute, 98 percent of US consumers who purchased plant-based meats also bought meat products. It's mostly meat-eaters supporting these processed vegan products. Not vegans.

So, to claim that it's unhealthy to be vegan because vegan convenience foods exist is simply a red herring. There isn't one way to be vegan, and whether you're vegetarian, pescetarian, vegan, or non-vegan, we *all* eat convenience foods, some more processed than others—unless you're living in your own private jungle and eating solely off of what grows on trees and vines.

Technically speaking, a "processed food" is any food that has been washed, cleaned, cut, milled, chopped, heated, pasteurized, blanched, boiled, cooked, canned, jarred, frozen, mixed, blended, or packaged. Essentially, any food that is in any way altered from its whole natural state is considered a "processed food."

That means the orange you squeeze into orange juice, the fresh blueberries you blend into a smoothie, or the peanuts you whip into peanut butter—are all processed foods. So are whole-grain bread, tofu, and hummus. So are potato chips, energy bars, and cereals. So are meat-based burgers, hot dogs, and chicken nuggets. So are plant-based burgers, hot dogs, and chicken nuggets.

There is a huge spectrum when we talk about "processed foods."

To help more easily and accurately distinguish between different points on this spectrum, a group of researchers came up with a way to categorize foods (and drinks) based on the extent and purpose of their processing. It's called the NOVA classification system and ranges from unprocessed and minimally processed foods and drinks to ultra-processed.[51] And so to talk about "vegan foods" being ultra-processed is to disregard these distinctions.

There is a huge difference between a bowl of fresh (or frozen) blueberries and a plate of vegan chicken nuggets. Putting minimally processed foods aside (nut butters, fruit smoothies, tomato sauce), there are certainly legitimate questions about whether or not more highly processed plant-based products are nutritionally and environmentally sound. And the answer is: they're always healthier and more eco-friendly. How *much* depends on what you're comparing them to.

- Compared to an Impossible Burger, a whole bean burger is healthier.
- Compared to a vegan chicken nugget, a bowl of blueberries is healthier.
- Compared to a plant-based hot dog, a carrot dog is healthier.

It's all relative, and that relativity applies to animal meats and milks versus plant-based meats and milks, as well.

- Compared to a meat-based hamburger, an Impossible Burger is healthier.
- Compared to a meat-based chicken nugget, a vegan chicken nugget is healthier.
- Compared to a meat-based hot dog, a plant-based hot dog is healthier.
- Compared to animal milks, plant-based milks are healthier.

Every single time.

This is also the case when you look at the environmental footprint of animal products and highly processed vegan products. Data analysts looking at the most environmentally friendly diets and products have concluded that "meat substitutes still have a footprint around ten times smaller than beef from the US or Europe. . . . Switch your beef burger for a Beyond Meat or Impossible Burger and you'll cut emissions by around 96 percent. And even the footprint of the world's lowest-carbon beef is still five times bigger than the Beyond Meat or Impossible Burger, and ten times bigger than Quorn."[52]

Ultimately, the holier-than-thou attitude about "processed vegan foods" distracts people from the real issues. The problems we're experiencing from a health, ethical, and environmental perspective are because of the breeding, killing, and consuming of animals and their secretions. We didn't get to where we are because of Beyond Sausages or Quorn Nuggets.

Vegan is not a diet. The specific ways people choose to eat under this umbrella called "vegan" or "plant-based" are *diets*: you can choose to eat no oil, no sugar, all fruit, no fruit, all whole foods, no soy, no wheat, no blue foods, only blue foods. Those are all *diets*: dietary choices you can make whether or not you're vegan.

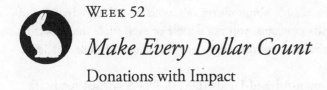

Make Every Dollar Count

Donations with Impact

While leveraging charitable donation write-offs in order to lower taxable income is a nice perk, most people donate to charity out of altruism. And if you do donate to charity, most likely you want your donations to have *impact*, to be used *effectively*, to have a positive and lasting effect on the causes you care about. Given the multitude of social issues seeking support, how do we decide where to donate? With over 1.5 million registered nonprofits in the United States alone, how do we choose? Here are some suggestions for making the most of your charitable contributions—whether you have $100 to donate or $100,000.

1. **Join the Effective Altruism Movement.** Effective altruism is a movement, a philosophy, a way of doing good in the world in the most effective way possible. It involves using evidence-based reasoning to determine the most effective ways to address social challenges, with the goal of achieving the greatest good for the greatest number of people.

2. **Consult Charity Evaluators.** GiveWell, Charity Navigator, GuideStar, and Animal Charity Evaluators are examples of nonprofits that help donors make informed decisions about organizations and causes they want to support.

3. **Take the 10 Percent Pledge.** The concept of *tithing* has its roots in the Old Testament practice of giving *one tenth* of one's income to support the priests and upkeep of the temple. It has long since expanded beyond religion and provides a model for people who want to increase their impact. You can do this on your own, or join effective-altruism-inspired organizations such as *Giving What We Can* to make a public pledge to donate a minimum of 10 percent of your income to organizations committed to making a positive, measurable difference in the world.

4. **Take Advantage of Matching Gifts Programs.** Many employers offer matching gift programs, where they match donations made by

employees to eligible nonprofit organizations. By taking advantage of matching gifts programs, you can double or even triple the impact of your contributions, maximizing the effectiveness of your charitable giving.

5. **Consider Donor-Advised Funds (DAFs).** Donor-advised funds are a flexible way to make donations to the charities you want to support. You set up a fund with a qualified financial institution or advisor, make an initial contribution of cash, assets, or investments, receive an immediate tax deduction, then dole out the "grants" over time, while your money also grows. Consult a financial advisor to see if this is right for you.

6. **Create Legacy Giving (Bequests).** Legacy giving involves including charitable donations in one's will, trust, or estate plan. Bequests can be specified as a percentage of your estate, a specific dollar amount, or as a residual beneficiary after other obligations have been met.

Finally, don't wait to introduce children to the practice of philanthropy. Making charitable donations from a young age instills in them the value of empathy, generosity, and community responsibility. Whether they're your own children, nieces and nephews, or godchildren, you can involve them in acts of giving at a young age, nurturing their understanding of the needs of others, empowering them to make a positive difference in the world, and encouraging a lifelong commitment to supporting the causes they care about.

Why I'm Hopeful

I've been an animal advocate for more than thirty years, and I see enough cruelty every day to have a pretty bleak view of the world. And yet I have hope.

No, I'm not a mythical creature. No, I'm not delusional. Yes, I'm paying attention.

And still, I have hope.

I have hope because I dwell on what I can solve rather than on what I can't.

I have hope because there's much to be hopeful about. History gives you great perspective if you just step back and heed the wisdom it imparts: we *have* done worse and we *can* do better. Both are true. Poet and philosopher George Santayana observed that "those who cannot remember the past are condemned to repeat it," but the first part of that maxim is equally true and rarely quoted: "Progress depends on retentiveness. When experience is not retained, infancy is perpetual." I have hope for the future because I observe the lessons of the past.

I have hope because outrage doesn't change the world. Vision and vigilance do—along with the political, technological, economic, and moral forces that drive progress forward.

I'm hopeful because I live in a democratic country. I can criticize elected officials, I can vote them out, and I can exercise my power and privilege to help those who have neither.

I'm hopeful because scientific advances and technological breakthroughs have the potential to reduce carbon emissions, mitigate the effects of climate change, restore habitats, transition us completely away from fossil fuels, and save billions of animals from misery and death.

I'm hopeful because I live in an economic system that empowers visionaries to test their innovations in the marketplace, offering me the *choice* to support companies and products that reflect my taste and ethics—and reject those that don't.

My hope is not complacent; it's provisional. It's the difference between wanting things to change and taking action to facilitate that change.

My hope is cultivated. I actively nurture and fervently foster hope to maintain perspective, create resilience, and spread compassion.

My hope is rooted in joy. We don't have to be angry all the time to demonstrate that we care. We don't have to be outraged to show that we're conscious. We can be acutely aware, actively engaged, politically minded, and still have hope.

My hope is not delusional; it's rooted in facts, science, reason, and statistics. It is neither naive nor unrealistic. It is a rational response grounded in the reality of human history. My hope is *defiant*, as Howard Zinn so poignantly observed:

> To be hopeful in bad times is not just foolishly romantic. It is based on the fact that human history is a history not only of cruelty but also of compassion, sacrifice, courage, kindness.
>
> What we choose to emphasize in this complex history will determine our lives. If we see only the worst, it destroys our capacity to do something. If we remember those times and places—and there are so many—where people have behaved magnificently, this gives us the energy to act, and at least the possibility of sending this spinning top of a world in a different direction.
>
> And if we do act, in however small a way, we don't have to wait for some grand utopian future. The future is an infinite succession of presents, and to live now as we think human beings should live, in defiance of all that is bad around us, is itself a marvelous victory.

I have hope, because I choose to. And I hope you do, too.

May you live in defiance of all that is bad around you and create a future from the infinite succession of presents. May it be so.

ACKNOWLEDGMENTS

I always say that the birth of a book has many midwives who bring it to life, and that is no exception here.

My literary agent, Leslie Stoker, tenaciously championed this book and ensured that it found the perfect home. My editor, Emily Turner, understood my vision and enhanced it with her keen insight and thoughtful suggestions.

My beloved husband, best friend, and biggest champion, David Goudreau, has not only supported me in the writing of this book but in the living of it. The embodiment of compassion, magnanimity, and generosity, David has joined me on every step of this journey and continues to inspire me to be a better person.

Though she died in 2020, my mother, Arlene Patrick, is infused throughout the pages of this book, both in the ways she consciously and unconsciously compelled me to live compassionately and in the ways that I'm sorry to have fallen short.

I'm profoundly grateful for the incredible people I have the honor of calling my friends, who lead their lives with purpose, joy, and compassion, making the world a better place by virtue of their place in it.

I deeply appreciate all of my book-readers, podcast-listeners, class-attendees, and devoted supporters who put their trust in me and my message. What a gift to be part of your journey.

My sense of purpose is renewed each and every day that I wake up to the animals I'm lucky enough to live among and live with. May I continue to learn from them what it means to live lightly on this Earth.

Where to send items for proper disposal or recycling:
- TerraCycle—terracycle.com
- Ridwell—ridwell.com
- Buy Nothing Project—buynothingproject.org
- Freecycle—freecycle.org
- Habitat for Humanity—habitat.org

Support for reducing or eliminating consumption of animal products:
- Meatless / Meat-Free Monday Campaigns—meatlessmonday.com
- The 30-Day Vegan Challenge—30dayveganchallenge.com
- Veganuary—veganuary.com
- NutritionFacts—nutritionfacts.org
- Food for Thought Podcast by Colleen Patrick-Goudreau—joyfulvegan.com/podcast
- Joyful Vegan—joyfulvegan.com

Plastic-free personal care products:
- Plaine Products—plaineproducts.com
- Ethique—ethiqueworld.com
- Lush—lush.com
- Bite—bitetoothpastebits.com

Nutritional supplements:
- Garden of Life—gardenoflife.com
- Vega—myvega.com
- Complement—lovecomplement.com
- Deva Nutrition—devanutrition.com

Ethical wildlife viewing:
- Animals Asia (Vietnam and China)—animalsasia.org
- Jane Goodall Institute's Chimp Eden (South Africa)—chimpeden.com
- Elephant Nature Park (Thailand)—elephantnaturepark.org
- Sheldrick Wildlife Trust (Kenya)—sheldrickwildlifetrust.org
- Dian Fossey Gorilla Fund (Rwanda)—gorillafund.org
- Marine Mammal Center (USA)—marinemammalcenter.org
- Chimp Haven (USA)—chimphaven.org
- Wildlife SOS (India)—wildlifesos.org
- Donkey Sanctuary (Ireland and UK)—thedonkeysanctuary.org.uk
- Elephant Haven (France)—elephanthaven.com
- Boon Lott's Elephant Sanctuary (Thailand)—blesele.org
- Alternative Wolf and Bear Park Black Forest (Germany)—baer.de
- GreenViet Langur Monkey Conservation Tour (Vietnam)—greenviet.org
- Trips with World Vegan Travel (Worldwide)—worldvegantravel.com

Eco-friendly cat litters:
- Feline Pine—felinepine.com
- Ökocat—healthy-pet.com/okocat
- Yesterday's News—purina.com/yesterdays-news
- PetSafe ScoopFree Premium Crystal Non-Clumping Cat Litter—pet safe.net
- World's Best Cat Litter—worldsbestcatlitter.com
- Nature's Logic—natureslogic.com
- sWheat Scoop—swheatscoop.com
- Cococat—cococat.shop
- Hempcat—hempcatlitter.com

Eco-friendly, nonanimal leather:
- Matt & Nat—mattandnat.com
- Stella McCartney—stellamccartney.com
- Arsayo—arsayo.com
- Doshi—doshishop.com
- Will's—wills-vegan-store.com
- Beyond Skin—beyondskin.co.uk
- Brave GentleMan—bravegentleman.com
- Mushroom Leather by MycoWorks—mycoworks.com
- Piñatex by Ananas Anam—ananas-anam.com

Books

Of course, I wholeheartedly recommend my cookbooks if you're looking for recipes, *The 30-Day Vegan Challenge* if you're looking for guidance on transitioning to veganism, and *The Joyful Vegan* for more on staying vegan healthfully and joyfully; in addition, here are some favorite books focused on the nutritional aspects of eating plant-based.

Barnard, Neal. *Dr. Neal Barnard's Program for Reversing Diabetes: The Scientifically Proven System for Reversing Diabetes Without Drugs.* Emmaus, PA: Rodale Books, 2018.

Campbell, T. Colin, and Thomas M. Campbell. *The China Study: The Most Comprehensive Study of Nutrition Ever Conducted and the Startling Implications for Diet, Weight Loss, and Long-term Health*, revised and expanded ed. Sanger, CA: American West Books, 2016.

Davis, Brenda, and Vesanto Melina. *Becoming Vegan: Comprehensive Edition: The Complete Reference to Plant-Based Nutrition.* Summertown, TN: Book Publishing Company, 2014.

Davis, Brenda, and Reshma Shah. *Nourish: The Definitive Plant-Based Nutrition Guide for Families—With Tips & Recipes for Bringing Health, Joy, & Connection to Your Dinner Table.* Deerfield Beach, FL: Health Communications, 2020.

Fuhrman, Joel. *The End of Heart Disease: The Eat to Live Plan to Prevent and Reverse Heart Disease.* San Francisco, CA: HarperOne, 2018.

Greger, Michael. *How Not to Die: Discover the Foods Scientifically Proven to Prevent and Reverse Disease.* New York: Flatiron Books, 2015.

Stone, Gene, ed. *Forks Over Knives: The Plant-Based Way to Health.* Illustrated edition, foreword by T. Colin Campbell. New York: The Experiment, 2011.

Introduction

1. Charles Darwin, *The Descent of Man, and Selection in Relation to Sex* (London: John Murray, 1871), chap. IV.

Weeks

1. US Environmental Protection Agency, "National Overview: Facts and figures on materials, wastes and recycling," 2023, www.epa.gov/facts-and -figures-about-materials-waste-and-recycling/national-overview-facts -and-figures-materials#NationalPicture.

2. Adriana Valcu-Lisman, "Per Capita Red Meat and Poultry Consumption Expected to Decrease Modestly in 2022," Economic Research Service, US Department of Agriculture, 2022, https://www.ers.usda.gov/data-products/ chart-gallery/gallery/chart-detail/?chartId=103767.

3. Hannah Ritchie, *Not the End of the World: How We Can Be the First Generation to Build a Sustainable Planet*, Kindle edition (New York: Little, Brown, 2024), 173.

4. Ibid.

5. Ibid.

6. Yang Yu and Edward C. Jaenicke, "Estimating Food Waste as Household Production Inefficiency," *American Journal of Agricultural Economics* (January 23, 2020), https://doi.org/10.1002/ajae.12036.

7. National Resource Defense Council, *Wasted: How America Is Losing Up to 40 Percent of Its Food from Farm to Fork to Landfill*, 2nd ed., 2017, https:// www.nrdc.org/sites/default/files/wasted-2017-report.pdf.

8. Ibid.

9. Gustavo Porpino, Juracy Parente, and Brian Wansink, "Food waste paradox: Antecedents of food disposal in low income households," *International Journal of Consumer Studies* 39, no. 6 (November 2015), https://online library.wiley.com/doi/abs/10.1111/ijcs.12207.

10. Landfill Methane Outreach Program (LMOP), "Basic Information about Landfill Gas," US Environmental Protection Agency (EPA), April 25, 2024, https://www.epa.gov/lmop/basic-information-about-landfill-gas.

11. K. Park, "The Role of Dietary Phytochemicals: Evidence from Epidemiological Studies," *Nutrients* 15, no. 6 (2023): 1371, https://www.ncbi.nlm.nih .gov/pmc/articles/PMC10054640/.

12. C. D. Michener, *The Bees of the World* (Baltimore, MD: Johns Hopkins University Press, 2007).

13. Laura Tangley, "The Truth about Honey Bees: Raising Nonnatives Does Not 'Save the Bees'—and May Harm Them," *Garden for Wildlife*, National Wildlife Federation, June 1, 2021.

14. "Understanding Neonicotinoids," Xerces Society for Invertebrate Conservation, https://www.xerces.org/pesticides/understanding-neonicotinoids, last updated 2024.

15. The Recycling Partnership, "2020 State of Curbside Recycling Report," 2020, https://recyclingpartnership.org.

16. US Environmental Protection Agency, "National Overview: Facts and Figures on Materials, Wastes and Recycling," 2020, https://www.epa.gov/facts-and-figures-about-materials-waste-and-recycling.

17. Environmental Protection Agency, "Facts and Figures about Materials, Waste, and Recycling Nondurable Goods: Product-Specific Data," 2023, https://www.epa.gov/facts-and-figures-about-materials-waste-and-recycling/nondurable-goods-product-specific-data#tab-6.

18. Hannah Ritchie, "Cars, Planes, Trains: Where Do CO_2 Emissions from Transport Come From?" OurWorldInData.org, 2020, https://ourworldindata.org/co2-emissions-from-transport.

19. Hannah Ritchie, "Which Form of Transport Has the Smallest Carbon Footprint?" OurWorldInData.org, 2023, https://ourworldindata.org/travel-carbon-footprint.

20. Ibid.

21. United Egg Producers, "US Egg Production and Hen Population," 2024, https://unitedegg.com/facts-stats.

22. Humane Society of the United States, "An HSUS Report: Welfare Issues with Selective Breeding of Egg-Laying Hens," https://www.humanesociety.org/sites/default/files/docs/egg-laying-hen-report.pdf, accessed October 11, 2024.

23. Andrea Collins, "Expiring Confusion about Food Date Label," National Resources Defense Council, May 9, 2023, https://www.nrdc.org/bio/andrea-collins/expiring-confusion-about-food-date-labels.

24. Anahad O'Connor, "New Dietary Guidelines Urge Less Sugar for All and Less Protein for Boys and Men," *New York Times*, January 7, 2016.

25. The United States Department of Agriculture (USDA), in collaboration with the US Department of Health and Human Services (HHS), sets nutritional guidelines.

26. Physicians Committee for Responsible Medicine, "Health Concerns about Dairy," 2024, pcrm.org/good-nutrition/nutrition-information/health-concerns-about-dairy.

27. See: "FoodData Central," US Department of Agriculture, Agricultural Research Service, 2024, https://fdc.nal.usda.gov/index.html.

28. Michael Clark et al., "Estimating the environmental impacts of 57,000 food products," *Proceedings of the National Academy of Sciences* 119, no. e2120584119 (2022).

29. Michael Greger, "Optimum Nutrient Recommendations," NutritionFacts.org, 2024, https://nutritionfacts.org/optimum-nutrient-recommendations/.

30. Organisation for Economic Co-operation and Development, *Global Plastics Outlook: Economic Drivers, Environmental Impacts and Policy Options*, OECD, February 22, 2022, https://doi.org/10.1787/de747aef-en.

31. Ritchie, *Not the End of the World*, 234.

32. Jeannie Evers, "Great Pacific Garbage Patch," *National Geographic*, April 10, 2024, https://education.nationalgeographic.org/resource/great-pacific-garbage-patch/.

33. Ritchie, *Not the End of the World*, 285.

34. Ibid.

35. J. F. Bos et al., "Energy use and greenhouse-gas emissions in organic and conventional farming systems in the Netherlands," *NJAS-Wageningen Journal of Life Sciences* 68 (2014): 61–70, https://doi.org 10.1016/j.njas.2013.12.003.

36. Ritchie, *Not the End of the World*, 63.

37. Dr. Michael Greger, "A 'Normal' Cholesterol Level Can Still Be Deadly," *Fortune*, December 5, 2023, https://fortune.com/well/2023/12/05/normal-cholesterol-level-deadly-michael-greger-how-not-to-age/.

38. See: "Homocysteine," Cleveland Clinic, 2024, https://my.clevelandclinic.org/health/articles/21527-homocysteine.

39. Greger, "A 'Normal' Cholesterol Level Can Still Be Deadly."

40. Kitty Block and Sara Amundson, "Good News! Washington Becomes 12th State to Ban Sale of Animal-Tested Cosmetics," Humane Society of the United States, March 19, 2024, https://www.humanesociety.org/blog/washington-state-cosmetics-animal-testing-sales-ban.

41. Mitch Jacoby, "Most of the glass dropped into recycling bins doesn't get recycled," *Chemical & Engineering News* 97, no. 6 (February 11, 2019).

42. T. Colin Campbell and Thomas M. Campbell II, *The China Study: The Most Comprehensive Study of Nutrition Ever Conducted and the Startling Implications for Diet, Weight Loss, and Long-Term Health* (Dallas, TX: BenBella Books, 2006).

43. Ritchie, *Not the End of the World*, 55.

44. Hannah Ritchie, "You Want to Reduce the Carbon Footprint of Your Food? Focus on What You Eat, Not Whether Your Food Is Local," OurWorldIn Data.org, 2020, https://ourworldindata.org/food-choice-vs-eating-local.

45. David Lightsey, "Are Organic Foods More Nutritious?," American Council on Science and Health, December 18, 2020, https://www.acsh.org/news /2020/12/18/are-organic-foods-more-nutritious-15225.

46. J. T. McGuirt et al., "Produce price savings for consumers at farmers' markets compared to supermarkets in North Carolina," *Journal of Hunger & Environmental Nutrition* 6, no. 1 (2011): 86–98.

47. T. McDaniel, F. Soto Mas, and A. L. Sussman, "Growing connections: Local food systems and community resilience," *Society & Natural Resources* 34, no. (2021): 1375–93.

48. J. Kerr and J. Landry, "Pulse of the Fashion Industry 2017," Global Fashion Agenda & The Boston Consulting Group, 2017, https://globalfashion agenda.org/pulse-of-the-industry/.

49. "Food Waste in America in 2024," Recycle Track Systems, 2024, https:// www.rts.com/resources/guides/food-waste-america/.

50. "Animal-focused nonprofit organizations," Cause IQ, 2024, https://www .causeiq.com/directory/animal-organizations-list.

51. Michael J. Gibney, "Ultra-Processed Foods: Definitions and Policy Issues," *Current Developments in Nutrition* 3, no. 2 (2019): nzy077, https://doi.org 10.1093/cdn/nzy077.

52. Ibid.

ABOUT THE AUTHOR

Photo by Michelle Cehn

Colleen Patrick-Goudreau, affectionately known as the Joyful Vegan, is a recognized expert and thought leader on the culinary, social, ethical, and practical aspects of living compassionately, healthfully, and sustainably. An award-winning author of seven books—including the best-selling *The Joy of Vegan Baking, The 30-Day Vegan Challenge*, and *The Joyful Vegan: How to Stay Vegan in a World that Wants You to Eat Meat, Dairy, and Eggs*—Colleen is also an acclaimed speaker, a regular contributor to National Public Radio, and the host of all-inclusive luxury vegan trips around the world. Producer of *Food for Thought* since 2006 (one of the longest-running podcasts), Colleen also cofounded the political action committee East Bay Animal PAC to work with government officials on animal issues in the San Francisco Bay Area. She lives in Oakland, California, with her beloved husband David, her treasured cat Michiko, and the memory of her much-loved and much-missed cat Charlie, who died during the production of this book. She can be found at JoyfulVegan.com.